POLKA-DOTS IN A CHECKERED LIFE

A collection of reflections, random conclusions
and occasional confusion

DarbyLee Patterson

Polka Dots in a Checkered Life
By Darby Lee Patterson
© 2024 Darby Lee Patterson
All Rights Reserved

BoltonRoadPublishing@gmail.com
MMXXIV
Bolton Road Publishing P.O. Box 556
Pollock Pines, CA 95726

ISBN: 979-8-218-46243-7

Acknowledgments & Foreword

Life happens, and suddenly, most of it lies in the past. This collection of columns I've written weekly for years reflects time, places, opinions, and adventures over decades. I'm hoping readers will enjoy the variety of memories and observations and that some will inspire thoughts and others inform or entertain.

I've valued the feedback I've gotten from subscribers to "Down Darby Lane" – my online blog. Readers' observations and personal stories inspired me to keep writing – even during weeks when, well, I just felt like moping or giving up. But I've been a writer for decades – first in radio and then as a newspaper publisher and reporter for publications throughout California. I feel a responsibility to rise above my lesser moments and deliver content to loyal readers who give me reasons to write. I dedicate this collection to them.

On a personal level, I'm hoping my children and grandchildren will learn to know me beyond our family ties – maybe smile and say, "She did what?"

Acknowledgments: With thanks to Karen Duncan for making me look better through proofing, editing, and being the smartest person in the room; to the people who trusted me with their stories; my husband, Randall, for always positive support; Murphy, my canine companion, for warming my heart throughout the process, and you for spending time on the pages that follow.

Table of Contents

PLACES

Safe in the Stacks

When I was a child in Winona, Minnesota, the public library was a prominent community resource. It was also one of the largest and most imposing buildings in the small river city – three beautiful stories of Neoclassical architecture. At first, there were weekly trips to the children's section to check out books with lots of pictures. Later, the adult section on the second story became so much more – a resource for school work, a place to flirt with a cute boy, and, for me, a refuge from mean-spirited she-bullies.

Many of the upper-level floors were made of solid glass blocks that let light filter through from below. There was a big common room with grand leather chairs and long, ornate wood tables. This room held reference books, multi-volume collections, and librarians putting a finger to their lips and hissing, "Ssshhhh…!" Altogether, it was a place of mystery with imposed silence, ringing echoes off marble walls, and safety.

The ambiance and experience of today's libraries are different. They've been replaced as the citadels of world knowledge by the digital age of information at our fingertips. I've noticed that librarians no longer scowl and "Ssshh.." at patrons for talking out loud. But in communities large and small, the library is still a public treasure, free and available to all.

It began about 2,360 years ago in Assyria. There, King Ashurbanipal made a library of 30,000 inscribed clay tablets available to subjects who were most likely scholars and scribes. (I'd guess there was no children's section.) Historians say the idea of saving information actually dates back about 5000 years, with stacks of one-inch clay tablets providing knowledge (and exercise) for some of our earliest accountants.

But for me, the most scintillating historical library is not in a faraway land, but smack-dab in the U.S. of A. It's the Darby Free Library, founded in 1743 in Darby, Pennsylvania. It was the innovation of 29 Quaker men. Better yet, it represented an early acknowledgment of female literacy. Of course, that only happened because Ann Paschall inherited a 'share' of the Darby Library and became the first female member. Alas, equality was not included in the transfer. She was barred from membership meetings and dismissed with the statement, "…her attendance at our meetings is dispensed with." I assume she also did not attend the members' burning of "The Pupil of Pleasure," a novel published in 1776 that included a touch of "seduction." Today, a first edition of the novel by Courtney Melmoth is for sale at $2,200.

But I digress. When I was young, it wasn't common to go to a bookstore, and Amazon had not yet been born. So, a trip to the library served many purposes. A quiet place to study, a resource for free books, an elegant building with high ceilings decorated like a topping on a birthday cake, a marble floor, and tall book stacks where getting lost was possible. The latter feature was my goal. Not really 'getting lost' but becoming very hard to find.

The hour after school was dangerous. It was when a gang of popular girls (I was not in that classification) gathered in the halls and made plans. I was often included in those plans – not as a participant, but as a target. I was prey in school hallways, the lunchroom, and (most dangerous of all) the girls' locker room for gym class. Once the school day was over and I'd successfully avoided the pack of she-teens, I ran for the public library next door to the school.

I favored the upper floor because it housed titles of little interest to junior high schoolers. While chilling in the stacks and waiting for the clique of girls to get bored and leave, I browsed the titles, read some pages. Chose a few books to check out when the coast was clear. I didn't know it then, but many years later, I realized they'd done me a favor.

It was the beginning of my life with words. Had I not been chased into the sanctuary of the library, I might have been off giggling with girls and flirting with boys. But no, I was surrounded by thousands of books that held secrets from places I'd never been, words I'd never before seen. I went away on adventures that authors made up and made real for me. For two very long years of hiding in the book stacks, I learned about storytelling, started writing, and never stopped.

For most of my working life, it was writing that rewarded me with paychecks – I was a news reporter for several outlets and eventually wrote a few books, including one for children that featured a gang of bully boys and girls and four amateur sleuths – each with a special need that made them targets for the gang. Of course, my protagonists rule the day because good deserves to triumph over evil. (I dedicated the book to the kids who taunted me). A few more books followed.

I think it's not unusual for the human spirit to prevail and rise above adversity. And I even feel a hint of gratitude for being chased

4

into the shelter of the library. After all, where would I be today without them?

Library Trivia:

- One of the most overdue library books in the world was returned after 122 years.

- The more popular genres in prison libraries are paranormal romance, young adult titles, and the Left Behind series.

- The Guinness Book of World Records holds the record for being the book most often stolen from public libraries.

- At the end of the 19th century, library work was considered to be too overwhelming for women, and in 1900, the Brooklyn Public Library Association proposed building "a seaside rest home for those who had broken down in library service."

- The Library of Congress was founded in 1800. With 164 million items (one is a book by me!) and 1,350 kilometers (*838 miles*) of bookshelves, it's the world's largest library.

Mighty Miss of Give and Take

Suffocating through the extreme heat of the past weeks, my mind drifted back to a different time and place when weather conditions were dramatically opposite those we now experience. I grew up in Winona, Minnesota, a small town skirting the Mississippi River. She is often referred to as "mighty" both for her power and for the 2,318 miles from source to final destination - the Gulf of Mexico. The Algonquin-speaking Native Americans named the river "Father of Waters" (misi-big, sipi-water), and it's earned its status in the family.

Those of us along her route had little concern about too much summer sun. Ours was fear of flooding that breached dikes, dams, and levees. The destructive power of the Mississippi threatened towns throughout its cross-country journey to the Gulf, and in 1927, it flooded 23,000 sq. miles, killing 250 people.

Growing up in a placid river town, solidly Midwest down to its soul, tornadoes, and floods were feared like wildfires and earthquakes are in America's far west. They also disrupted the monotony of everyday life for teenagers trapped in a culture where routine and politeness are core values.

I was a senior in high school, stuck in a too-small house, and bored to tears when a massive storm hit our corner of the state. Word spread that the Mississippi threatened to flood its banks, and volunteers were needed. Over protests from my grandmother that I would probably drown, I ran through the rain to the Salvation Army Center, where we piled into white vans that ferried us to the edge of danger and the peak of excitement.

Rain poured down like it was dropping from buckets instead of clouds. We scurried from the vans to tents where Salvation Army people in wet blue uniforms barked orders and handed us sandwiches and little cartons of chocolate milk to deliver to voluntary crews filling sandbags, hoisting them over their shoulders, and racing to stack them like bricks onto the steep riverbank. The rain was so relentless that, throughout the afternoon, we could see the river rising over the newly laid sandbags.

The downpour kept us drenched. Umbrellas and raingear were useless. Throughout the day, we listened to the squawk and crackle of shortwave radios that issued continued dire warnings. It was a 12-hour day of excitement and purpose and not being stuck in the house.

On the trip back to home base, we listened intently as the van's driver (a Captain in the 'Army') regaled us about the virtues of his rank and ride. He said the van was nearly "unstoppable." That even Civil Defense "wouldn't dare" try. He demonstrated the features of the flashing lights on the dashboard and cranked up the siren for us. All the while, the windshield wipers frantically tried to keep up with the pounding rain. For a naive and bored teenager, it was exhilarating.

Although they called the event a "500-year flood," the Mississippi frequently exerts its awesome power. And it doesn't take a disaster for people living under her reign to bow in homage to her swift, unpredictable currents. As I grew up in her presence, I learned to think of her as a deity of nature – at once life-giving and life-taking. Most of us lost a friend to her dark underwater torrents. Sometimes it was a ski boat screaming along the ribbon of river that flew out of control, taking a young life in the pursuit of fun. Other times, the river claimed one of ours without explanation.

I recall when the older sister of a boy (who was an object of my admiration) died in an accident so unlikely that it defied understanding. An anchor rope on the family's boat caught up on a submerged object, and the young girl reached over the side to cut the rope with a fishing knife. The knife slipped from her grasp, hit a wave, bounced back, and severed her 17-year-old jugular vein.

Indeed, the river gave many of us our first experience with death. It caused us to doubt our faith, to think in puzzling philosophical ways when we would have preferred planning what to wear to the Friday night dance. But the Mississippi was a neighbor with multiple personalities. She gave us endless hours of recreation; took us to sandbars where we experienced the rites of youthfulness miles away from authoritative adults. It was there that we tested our upbringing, our solid Midwest virtues drummed in by no-nonsense parents.

The river was freedom. She was adventure. In winter, we skated across her milky white surface. We laughed, raced, twirled, and fell in puppy love. And in some of those years, a skater broke through the crystalline surface and drowned.

In the summers, she gave us boating, skiing, and fishing, a kiss on a sandbar – more growth, discovery, and loss. But random displays of dominance are never enough for the Mississippi, and from time to time, she delivers mass destruction lest we forget who is in charge.

Those devastated by the dissonant concert of sky and earth are not surprised. We never doubted the power of a great river to give and to take away. There is no truce with Mother Nature. We have no bargaining chips, no favors to call in, no power plays. We may not lose, but we will never win.

Magic, Music, and the Mediterranean

It was a dream trip. A cruise around the Mediterranean with stops in ports I thought I'd only read about in glossy magazines. And though I have memories of remarkable places such as Pompeii, Mallorca, and the Barbary Macaques of Gibraltar, the experience that remains most indelible is time spent on the ship. I traveled with my then-boyfriend and a young man, trying to forget a lost loved one.

She wasn't a floating city with multiple decks and thousands of travelers. Ours was a Greek ship with three floors above the water and rooms for the crew and employees on the deck below the waterline. It was more like a small town than a metropolis of vacationers. Over the period of our two weeks at sea, we became familiar with each other, sharing a few words, clinking toasts over dining tables set with the ship's signature china and silverware.

I became fast friends with the Romanian musicians – a portly, short accordion player, a lanky, nearly bald violinist, and a guitarist with a permanent smile for everyone. We invited them to our table many times, and as a music lover, singer, and fellow violinist, I made it to their list of favorite fans. They taught me some Romanian words and invited me to visit them in their homeland. We exchanged addresses.

Dinner was also a time to check out fellow travelers, to sum up their lives and relationships, to watch who drank too much of what, and also to estimate the cost of the elegant gowns worn by the women. The best up-close look was in the women's restroom, where the wall of mirrors was the main attraction. It was there that I spied an elegant, tall woman who floated in wearing a simple, understated black evening dress, her ash blonde hair confidently pulled back and highlighting the face of a one-time model. Not a fashion model, I thought. Perhaps an artist's mannequin. High cheekbones, large eyes the color of the Mediterranean, and porcelain skin delicately lined by time. She wasn't smiling, but there was a look of pleasure and disconnect on her face. A simple strand of diamonds shot off tiny sparks of brilliance. She wore no rings.

She didn't bother to look into the mirrors but went about her business. I waited for her, for another glance. When she emerged from the stall, she went to wash her hands and turned. For a brief moment and with no exchanged expression, we caught each other's eyes. The most interesting person on the ship, I decided.

Later that moonlit night, people migrated to the dance club, where a jazz band played standards to bring guests out on the floor. At 50-something, I was among the younger women on the ship. And, after marching around on dirt and gravel at historic sites throughout the day, many of the wives were unwilling or unable to step out on the dance floor. But the older men who knew how to guide a partner skillfully around the dance floor were eager to foxtrot and waltz and display their grace. And, by default, they chose me. I did not decline a single invitation.

Eventually, my party migrated to the ship's lounge and that's where my most vivid memory of the voyage lives forever. The lights were dim, and the atmosphere subdued. The accordion player was at the keys of a baby grand piano, sending out love notes. Couples leaned across small round tables and made promises to each other in whispers. We enjoyed a glass or two of wine. The fiddler and guitarist joined their colleague, and then the trio turned to me, gesturing for me to join them. I figured I'd had enough wine to make that possible. There, abandoning my fears and knowing I'd never see any of the people in the room again, I sang Maleguena in Spanish, backed by Romanian musicians on a Greek ship.

We ended to a round of applause, and I glided back to my table on a cloud. I sat down and accepted the glass of Greek wine someone sent over for me. That's when she walked from the dark end of the bar to our table, leaned over, and placed a swan-like hand next to mine. I smelled jasmine and whiskey. I looked up. She wore a hint of a smile. "My dear," she said and paused, "If it was my week for girls, I'd choose you." She rose like a monarch and drifted out the door.

The Parthenon, the Vatican. The Prado. All those famed port stops are faded like old postcards, while the colors of that evening when mystery met magic on a moonlit sea are bright as day.

Escape to the Neolithic

I've been drowning in the complexities and work of selling, buying, and moving our household for many weeks. I needed an escape and, lacking the time and funds to jet off to somewhere marvelous, I visited some images of trips I'd taken in the past. A journey to my grandfather's homeland in England (taken years ago when travel seemed possible) took me way, *way* back in time and made my present condition (stranded and overworked) more bearable. So – come with me down my Memory Lane:

I hadn't planned to visit Avebury on the most auspicious day of the year, but there I was, on a sun-drenched dawn of the Summer Solstice. Most people know about Stonehenge, but Avebury is actually older – a favorite of locals and mystics, tourists, and young people dressed in flowing robes. Women with ropes of flowers in their hair.

Across the great swath of verdant green and along dirt pathways, people wandered freely. They sat in the grass, leaning against

Neolithic standing stones as sheep grazed, undisturbed by human company. Some of the visitors had spent the night at Avebury, awaiting the rising sun and the spark of imagination that might transport them far back in time, watching for the moment when the sun would strike the standing stones of Avebury and cast shadows as they have for more than 4500 years. Like those ancients, worshiping the forces of nature that framed the sky so perfectly at just this time of year.

At the same time, I was struck by the contrast of this experience. In America, our monuments are fenced off, paths restricted, treasures guarded by the sharp eyes of security personnel. In Avebury, a gentleman who was himself somewhat 'ancient' wore a blue blazer and talked modestly about his role as security detail – a job he did as he tended to other duties in the tiny village. People strolled unimpeded by barriers throughout the ancient site, touching, some kissing, the magnificent standing stones. Such behavior in the U.S. would get reprimands, warnings, removal.

Avebury is in the southern part of England, off the beaten path and near quiet villages that live peacefully amid the ghosts of Neolithic (the last Stone Age) society. These early human groups worshiped the many forces of nature that continue to draw people dabbling in mystical, spiritual, and alternative beliefs – along with archeologists who dig for more evidence and understanding of the generations that built Avebury.

Picture a large circle of 98 stones - about a mile in circumference, erected on a mound with a deep ditch along its inner rim. Today, only 27 stones remain. There are four openings to the circle at the primary compass points. Inside the circle are two more circles, each holding about 30 standing stones. Countless stones were destroyed over time as Christians in about 1100 sought to demolish Pagan worship and as nearby 17th-century villages raided the site for convenient building materials.

In 2003, a geophysical survey by the National Trust made a remarkable discovery. Near stones that were missing entirely, they found buried megaliths. At least 15 of the great stones lay under mounds of earth inside the circle. Using computer imagery, researchers hope to reconstruct just where each stone once stood before it was toppled and left to time.

The construction of Avebury required centuries of labor. With the lifespan of Neolithic peoples estimated at just 40 years, the baton of responsibility for the enormous project passed through many generations. Over the span of 600 years or so, the vision and passion persevered until one day, Avebury was one of Britain's greatest monuments – some people believe it to be the foremost Neolithic site in all of Europe.

In its present form, Avebury remains breathtaking and mind-bending. Many of the standing stones were moved to the site from more than two miles away - each weighing 40 tons and more. It remains a mystery how the early architects and their minions, minus the invention of the wheel, moved the Sarsen stones to the sacred site. (Sarsen stone is made of densely packed quartz that resists weather and time – thus, ideal for monument-making.) The stones are estimated to range from nine to twenty feet tall. Somehow, over the centuries, early Britons quarried, chipped, moved, and erected some 200,000 tons of mega-stones. There are, of course, numerous theories that range from rolling rocks on logs to aliens dropping them from outer space. But standing in the spell of Avebury, such academic quandaries seem irrelevant. The place is simply a tribute to the ingenuity of humankind.

Although much of what was once a central point of worship for England's earliest inhabitants has been destroyed, enough remains at Avebury to spark the imagination and stir the soul. That was certainly apparent on Summer Solstice as I watched dreamy-eyed young adults roam the wide-open site. On the top of a knoll, framed by the bright azure sky, a man and woman, both in business attire,embraced. The sheep, as if respecting the moment, turned their backs on them.

How the builders and visionaries of Avebury used the site continues to be debated. There is a belief (and evidence) of astronomical alignment, although it is not as clear as the alignment of Stonehenge with the sun, moon, and stars. Mystery surrounds the site and inspires imagination. Who were those early explorers? How did they devise technologies to move immovable stones over rugged miles of terrain? Early engineers, explorers, spiritual leaders who left us with a monumental mystery.

Memories like these put my current complaints about the downside of moving a bunch of boxes in perspective. I'll soon forget this pain, but I'll always remember Avebury.

Homeland of the Heart

I went back home for the long holiday weekend. It's curious to me that North Fork, "The exact geographical center of California," is not where I was born and raised, yet is the homeland of my heart. It's where I landed after shunning an academic future to run away with a wild man in a repurposed orange school bus. It's where I couldn't find a job from which I would not be fired, and so, made my own – a little tabloid newspaper I named *The Timberline Times* that celebrated life in a logging town, the folks in the one café on Main Street and the rowdy bar with "The world's biggest urinal."

In North Fork, I discovered that I loved writing, writing about people, for people. That I had a flair for graphic design and a determination to beat the odds. And the inspiration for my move from unemployed college graduate to struggling newspaper owner was a town steeped in history and abundant with personality.

When I eventually left North Fork, I was able to transform my publishing experience into a career as a journalist and writer. But the experience of my years immersed in the distinctive culture of the lumber and mining town, with its memorable characters – old-timers, young rebels, business owners barely hanging on, the Mono people struggling for respect, the acceptance of folks not fitting the norm – stayed with me. It became the setting for my mystery novel, *"The Song of Jackass Creek,"* and led me to think about the people and place throughout the many months of writing the book.

So, I was thrilled to have those memories reignited throughout the past July 4th weekend at the 61st Annual Loggers Jamboree. There, I found the spirit of North Fork had traveled the decades with descendants of people I knew and newcomers who carry on the culture - proof for me that I'd not romanticized the town's embedded character.

The arena for logging competitions was set up for axe throwing, double hand bucking, choker setting, hand chopping, tree falling, hot-power saws, log rolling, and more – all skills once needed and honed when logging was the lifeblood of North Fork. The mix of competitors was a warm country stew – young, old, men, women, members of the local Mono community. The star of the professional event was Nate Hodges, a national champion whose biceps resemble those of ancient Olympians carved in bronze. He went home with several top honors.

But enthusiasm for all the competitors was abundant and loud. Saws screamed for two hot days. Axes tumbled toward targets that rewarded the best shot with an explosion of beer from a can embedded in the center of the target. Through it all, families sat under pine trees, whistled, shouted, cheered, and celebrated a tradition that predates them all.

An accidental crowd favorite was a woman competing in axe throwing. She hefted the axe over her head and behind her back and strode mightily forward to gain momentum for the 20-foot throw. The axe tumbled through the air, barely missed the target, but squarely hit a 12-pack of Budweiser sitting on the ground. The explosion was loud, messy, and got a thunder of applause.

Above the arena, vendors sold local art, crafts, and food. Most popular was the big tent where legendary "Indian Tacos" had people lined up throughout the day. Individual pieces of puffy fried dough are layered with beans, cheese, seasoned meat, greens, and magic that only happens in the hands of one extended family. Each order is handmade, and I watched both days as folks walked back to their seats carrying their Indian Taco as if it was blown glass on a pillow.

I spent my days running between my booth (where I sold many books and donated others to local groups) and the arena, where I took photos. The best part, though, was talking to people – new and old friends: Courtney, a neighbor vendor who kindly helped me wrestle with my new pop-up tent that, of course, did not just pop up; a Mono Elder artist (Po-chi-chi-ca) whose memories reached back through many generations, before rancherias and reservations; enthusiastic members of the local history club who freely shared their knowledge with me, and people I'd known from my own days as a local. There was Tom Wheeler (now a County Supervisor), who has the distinction of being the oldest competitor to win the title of Top Logger at a previous Jamboree; the very perky Connie Carpenter from whom I rented my first office for *the Timberline Times*, and Candi Lewis, a Mono woman whose family makes beautiful dream catchers and walking sticks. I'll leave you with this story from her – and my own takeaway from the weekend: Home is where your heart is.

The Beast Inside the Beauty

July is just around the bend of our country road. Up here at the 4000-foot elevation, we're under an umbrella of tall pines, and it's the hard start of fire season. Some of you might remember that we were evacuated last fall when the Caldor Fire threatened thousands of homes throughout our niche of the Sierra. When we returned, we confronted evidence of how close the fire came to our quiet neighborhood that's home to more trees than people.

Powdery ash dusted our property. Black orbs the size of golfballs were scattered on our deck – large cinders from the fire that had flown on the wind and landed – many carrying live embers. We pictured them floating onto our roof, our 100-foot-tall cedars, and landing on wooden decks – each one carrying a spark. But still, we were safe and only facing some cleanup and repairs.

We live across the street from a winding trail through the forest that leads to a much-loved lake and recreation area. None of the sprawling hillside has been thinned for fire safety. Many nearby neighbors ignore the call to make properties 'hardened' for fire. And there are so many acres of public lands that it's not humanly possible for crews to thin and treat it all.

After the evacuation was lifted, many families listened to the siren's call and put their homes on the market. The fear of losing homes and possessions propelled them out of the mountains to the relative safety of lower elevations. We never considered leaving, and I want to tell you a bit about why.

It's well after dark, and I'm out in our backyard looking up at an inky sky that glitters with rhinestone stars. The Milky Way stretches above me in an arc – like a road that might lead to another world beyond my imagination. On the southern horizon, I see a golden moon, its peaks and valleys etched like a topo map floating in space. It's deeply quiet; even the birds are nested down and waiting for dawn. I remember the last evening we'd spent in the valley – dining outdoors with a friend. Walking back to our car, my husband and I looked up. Not one star to be seen in an artificially illuminated sky, and the moon was a sickly pale version of the one that hovers over our mountain home.

The next morning, we leash up two supremely excited small dogs and walk a winding route through our neighborhood. Homes are built on large lots – mostly a third to a half-acre. Pine trees stand like sentinels, giving people a sense of privacy and freedom. It's a hilly path that gives us a couple miles of exercise and a chance to breathe in sweet, clean mountain air. I remember stopping to give my buddy Murphy a chance to sniff at pine duff that clearly indicated the presence of something fascinating – like a squirrel or a coyote, skunk, rabbit, or a flock of wild turkeys. I listened to the sound of – nothing. No planes in the sky, TVs blaring, machines running. We walked our two miles and didn't once encounter a car driving on the street. It was quiet, like the breath of a sleeping infant.

Home to breakfast with a small table that looks out on a vacant, treed lot and a street that carries more walkers than cars. From this ground-level watch tower, we're entertained daily by a wide variety of birds and fat squirrels whose visits are encouraged with full feeders. Occasionally, we glimpse a special critter like a deer or an eagle. There are also mountain lions and brown bears that prowl mostly at night. And this year, I had a ringside seat to magic. Two Steller Jays built a nest of twigs under the eave atop a drain pipe above our kitchen window. I watched them make repeated trips until it was time to sit. The female warmed the eggs, and the male flew back and forth with food for his mate and extra twigs to add to the nursery. A few weeks later, when Mom and Pop were gone, I spotted two tiny yellow beaks popping up from the rubble nest. And day by day, I saw more of them until the day they stood up on spindly legs, flapped their tiny wings, and made me happy for the rest of the day. Within a week, the nest was empty, and I started spotting the youngsters at my feeders, their new feathers shining like blue lapis in the sun.

Some days, we take longer hikes – out our front door, across the street, and down the steep hill. The path we walk leads to Jenkinson Lake, a beautiful spot that's serene on weekdays and bustling with campers on weekends. But our path is a local secret and always quiet. Weeks ago, we heard a rumbling down in the ravine that abuts the path, where a tiny stream runs in the springtime. A chocolate-brown bear was scampering up the hill on the far side, eager to escape from humans and schnauzers. On another hike to the lake, a large red fox made an Olympic leap across our path and vanished into the woods.

These everyday occasions and personal moments with Mother Nature explain why so many of us remain in our mountain homes despite a close encounter with her most lethal weapon. It's the sounds, the lack of sounds, the being snowed-in with a woodfire for comfort, watching dogwood trees explode with blossoms, finding the damp footprint of a mountain lion in the morning. It's a silent agreement to accept both the blessings and the perils of our chosen environment.

Fire on the Mountain,
Angst in the Air

I'm writing to you today with a new unwanted title – Fire Refugee. Yesterday morning, we awoke to a dark cloud covering our eastern horizon. It was evident, as we took the dogs for their morning walk, that the Caldor Fire was approaching our little haven in the mountains. We returned home and began slowly packing things we'd put aside just in case one of the many fires burning in our region came too close. Within the hour, that precautionary move became mandatory. Officials sent out their Red Flag warning that our community would have to quickly evacuate.

First, into the truck - what was really needed for us and our dogs. Then, sentimental things that are irreplaceable. The 1920s black and white photo of my grandparents in its oval brass frame. A large painting done by my 6-year-old grandson and his dad. A portrait of myself by a noted painter whose work hangs in museums (and served to embarrass my son during family dinners). I ripped some family photos off the walls and grabbed my violins and Irish flute.

At 11 in the morning, we joined a chain of cars and trucks heading down a winding four-mile road to the nearby freeway, a trip that usually takes about eight minutes. It was an hour before we saw the fast lane to safety. We landed at the vacant home of a family member who immediately offered us shelter. We are anxious, tired, safe, and grateful.

In an odd and unfortunate way, our August emergency does not seem as overwhelming as it might be when taken into greater perspective. Consider (as I know you are) the relentless pandemic. A doomsday report from the United Nations specifically detailing how life as we know it is over. Countless thousands of families in Afghanistan surrounded by terror and fear at the hand of humankind. People in Haiti struggling to endure the most violent acts of nature. We all react to what we've been given to bear in order to just survive.

Under such intense and extraordinary pressures, handling so many things well out of our control takes a toll. Before the last 18 months descended, I only had a vague understanding of anxiety. But now, thoughts about what could happen, what might happen, filter through my mind unbidden. This unwanted voice becomes loud enough to drown out far more useful thoughts – like where did I leave the car keys, where are my glasses. Did I shut off the stove?

I'll walk with purpose out of one room and into another without the vaguest idea of what I meant to do. Of course, at a certain age, one wonders if this is some foreboding of mental decline. But, thankfully, Google has this issue covered, and the culprit is Cortisol.

High anxiety conjures up this hormone in excess. While healthy levels enhance memory, an overload has the opposite effect. With so much worry about so many things – from health to weather, war, and peace, and thanks to the UN report, a glimpse of a gradual apocalypse - Cortisol shows up to help us deal with imminent danger. It crowds out practical memory to make us ready to 'fight, flight, or freeze' in the face of danger. It's not me or you that's failing to remember what we were doing – it's human evolution and survival kicking in.

I checked all that out in exile at our temporary home today, awaiting the next move from an unpredictable fire. So, rather than move on to searching online for more fire updates, I decided to stop and write to you. The act of sitting down and thinking, creating a thoughtful message that I can share with you, puts me back in control of that hormone, looking for a reason to shoplift my brain. The same is true for me when I sit down with clay and make something with my hands – concentrating on a vision that I can make into a sculpture with work and time. Or when I use my modest talents to help a community effort reach its goal. It's not things I do, but why I do them. It's personal for me, as it is for you. When I'm engaged in my here and now, I'm temporarily free of the intangible 'maybe' that bursts to life with anxiety.

Dr. Robert McCarron, a psychiatrist and professor at U.C. Irvine, says this approach can help us quell anxiety – even in this 'Age of Anxiety. "Between current foreign affairs, raging fires, and a seemingly unending pandemic, life can be especially difficult. Now is a time to care for ourselves, loved ones, and even strangers," he says. "One way is to monitor our mood, sleep, nutrition, and physical activity. And, consider looking for even small ways in which we can add goodness for our family, friends, neighbors, and society."

We can take conscious actions to get ourselves grounded when anxiety seems overwhelming and when that helpful hormone turns harmful. I'm telling myself this as we face the prospect of an angry fire consuming our home, reducing our community to ashes. And thankfully, with effort, I'm able to see this personal threat in the context of what others in our roiling world must endure. Perspective helps. Writing for you helps.

Hello, this is Mother Earth;
Is anyone listening?

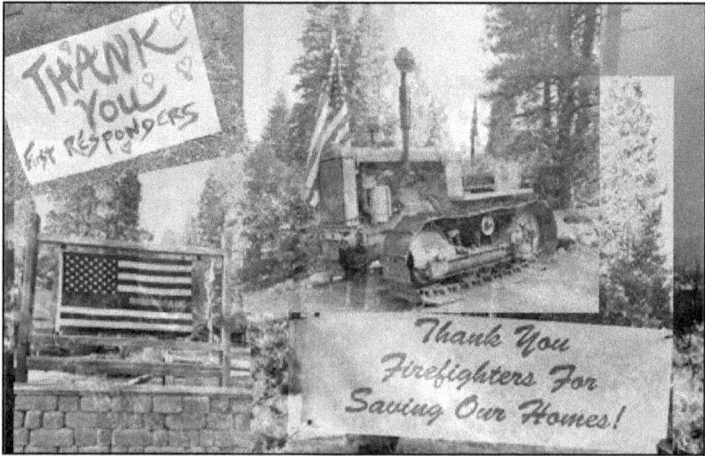

It's been 23 days since the start of the Caldor Fire. Up here on the mountain where so many of us moved to live in clean air amid the majesty of towering pines, life took an unwelcome (yet not unexpected) turn. We went from watching for deer grazing on someone's summer garden, bears sampling the delights of garbage cans, and the occasional mountain lion slinking through someone's yard to closing windows to air quality that was hazardous to breathe and, finally, evacuation from an active fire.

Returning home about three weeks later, some of us got lucky and tackled minor problems – dead refrigerators with rotting food and layers of ash covering every outdoor surface, wilted vegetable gardens we'd planted in the spring. But so many others lost their homes and remain refugees from the rural life they knew and loved. For them, there's no coming home to clean up and move on.

How we handle destruction and displacement is a personal matter – and may be related to the severity of trauma that we suffer. Me? Well, I kept busy and tried to do something productive every day. But when we headed back up the hill to resettle, I felt something stirring inside, and when we stopped for gas at a local station, I witnessed the same happening with someone else. A fire vehicle was parked at a nearby pump, and a woman waiting for her tank to fill walked up to the truck and thanked the three firefighters inside. They responded by saying how much they appreciate the support of the people they serve. She then touched the dusty red paint on the truck's door. "Thank you. Thank you from the very depth of our souls," she said, sobbing through the moment. "I'm sorry," she said, "I'm not usually a crier."

And that simple statement touched the protected part of me. We want to feel. Need to feel. Yet must stand strong to believe and survive. The feelings bubble to the surface in unexpected ways, and we must acknowledge that life as we knew it has changed. And that's sad, concerning, and necessary if we are to remain compassionate human beings.

In California, official fire season begins in September and lasts throughout the fall – often to November. California is a tinder box this year. Bone dry. Those of us who have already endured an active fire know that we cannot relax. We have to think about once again rifling through our homes and, choosing what we cannot lose and saying goodbye to the rest as we pull away to safety. From now till our first rain or dusting of snow, we hold our collective breath.

The experience of evacuation and abandoning the precious artifacts of our lives is never forgotten, as Joy, one of my readers, shared. "Last year, my husband and I had to evacuate our home of over forty years due to fires here in Oregon. There was little time to decide what to take and what to leave. The cat and dogs were our first concern, then birth certificates and other important documents," she wrote. ".... With horses, a cow and calf, chickens, dogs, and cats, it was a mad scramble to design a plan to protect all the living things and ourselves. Each time we located a route away from the fires, it closed. That was the longest day and night of my life."

Ironically, Joy was no stranger to fire. "I was a volunteer firefighter for 27 years," she said. "Wildfire is a whole different animal than structure fires. I understand house fires and the like, but wildfire tends to have a demon of its own. We humans can't usually stand against a monster."

And Joy offered some advice based on experience. "Be nice to yourself, and don't expect more than you can reasonably deal with just now. Don't dwell on the things left behind if you can avoid it. That will only increase your anxiety." Today, Joy's son is fighting the fires on the Kiwi Complex in Oregon, and she asks us to keep him and others in our thoughts. "Perhaps when you feel anxious, you will consider praying for all those men and women on fires. ... They have been away from home for extended periods of time," she says. "Mentally, the burdens they are carrying this year are back-breaking."

Because this is the world we've made due to unsound forestry practices, more natural disasters have already descended. A growing fire in our treasured Sequoia trees in the Giant Forest of Sequoia National Park is now a fire-fighting priority. I remember when I lived near those gems in the forest – then touted as nearly immune from wildfires. But not from those we are now seeing – hotter, bigger, and angrier than ever before. The majestic General Sherman Tree dominated the forest for up to 2,700 years and is widely touted as the "largest living thing on Earth." Today, it's threatened.

Already more than 1.54 million acres of forests have been charred, and fire season has only begun. Southern California is on high watch because legendary Santa Ana and Diablo winds blow hard in the fall. One fire captain said those winds will be pushing flames "like a freight train."

So, in America's West, we wait for time to pass – for gentle rains. For winter. But most importantly, we wait for a plan to repair a damaged earth that's sending us all a loud and urgent message. Will we wake up, listen, and act? Roll up our sleeves, change, and sacrifice before there's no turning back?

Requiem of Hope
for the Mountain

Up here, where a forest fire drove entire communities from their homes nine months ago, we're approaching warm weather and dire predictions of extreme dangers throughout the summer. Nonetheless, most of us have settled back in – maybe in denial based on a flawed belief that lightning can't strike twice. Our neighborhood trees have erupted with optimistic green. Purple irises stand like beauty queens, and California gold poppies shout enthusiastically from the hillsides.

As I write this, I look out through tall pines at a brilliant blue eastern sky – the same view that was billowing charcoal clouds of smoke last August – a sighting that sent us fleeing to safety in the valley and toting everything we felt necessary and important from our mountain home.

Spring also sings to us with the songs of birds returning from their winter homes – I've got a blue jay nest tucked under the eaves of my house. I've watched the pair make a nest worthy of an architect, protect their eggs for weeks, and just yesterday, I saw the tiny beaks of two fledglings pop up from their straw and twig castle. Snow white blossoms on the dogwoods have opened wide to the sun, and, like them, we've embraced a season that brings both threat and promise to all of us who returned home from the fire anxious, afraid, and uncertain.

But dozens of residents in the realm of the Caldor Fire have chosen to flee forever. Loud and bright 'For Sale' signs decorate our winding streets. The homes are selling in record time, but many are purchased by folks wealthy enough to buy vacation homes and visit only when sunshine and safety are forecast.

Most of us have taken short trips into our beloved high country – places where peaked mountains cradle small glaciers year-round. Where we go hiking in wilderness solitude and breathe air untainted by human inventions. But much of that precious environment bears the raw scars of the Caldor Fire, reminding us that nature does not bounce back as fast as humankind. My neighbor, Nicki, who has lived up here for decades, chose last weekend to jump on her motorbike and visit places she and her family have cherished for decades. She posted her observations on FaceBook and captured the charred landscape left by the fire that swept through Mother Nature's finest work:

"Everyone up here endured the Caldor Fire in their own way. We spent 18 days in a 'drug' apartment in Sacramento while we waited for news of our safe haven, our home, our beloved forest, and our ski mountain. We bought our first home together here when we married … our babies were born and raised here. The fire raged on indiscriminately. Everyone lost some. Some lost all."

"Mormon Emigrant Trail opened soon after we returned home. For 24 years, it's been our gateway to adventure and our sacred coming-home. I saw the destruction alone, on my bike, for the first time today on a solo ride through this land that I love. It's hard to put into words the guttural loss of the heartbeat of our forest. Many have posted photos of the moonscape that remains. I chose not to look at those photos but to see it in my own time with my own eyes. And I choose not to post my own gaping panoramic photos of the loss that reverberates in my soul …. for you will all see it in your own time, with your own eyes. You all … will try, just like I am today, to imagine a time when the woods will again be a riot of color, and the trees will grow and shelter new life. In the meantime, you might cry buckets, and it's ok. I did, and through tears came healing and, eventually, the newness of rebirth that, in its own time, would seem like the magic of what you never knew was missing. But today it's hard to picture … and it's hard to process … and that's ok, too."

Nicki has the power to evoke a range of emotions – from tears to gales of laughter. She writes uncensored, from the heart. In this post, she captured what keeps us up here despite history and made us aware of dire predictions of what's to come. It's undiminished hope. Untethered connection to place and sacred memories. The sounds of scrambling squirrels and night sightings of mountain lions, bear, and deer. Nothing to be afraid of; so we remain. We believe in the shimmering of light through the dogwoods. The forever cascade of stars that dance in our inky night sky. The quiet that's punctuated by bird songs and music made by wind through towering cedars. Despite the fire that drove us away last fall and threatens us on the cusp of another summer, it's all still here for us to know as home.

Island Hopping for Survival

Mitos Suson spent her childhood surrounded by threats and deprived of her father, who was a political prisoner in one of Philippine dictator Ferdinand Marcos's infamous prisons. Her once-privileged family lost most of their wealth, and she grew up in a prolonged crisis. She didn't know it then, but that traumatic period of childhood and adolescence not only left scars but also embedded a resiliency that became the foundation of her life – with highs and lows that might have sent many of us into permanent hiding.

Her journey to a better life landed her in Northern California, where she explored her talents, met her husband, and moved to the

Sierra foothills to work, write, and caretake 25 acres of rolling hills and pine trees. Quiet, serene, and isolated. But she kept in touch with her close-knit network of siblings and a large extended family of relatives on the islands of her birth, where kinship is sacred. Throughout Mitos's world travels, her heart remained in the Philippines with its timeless culture and traditions.

In 2017, Mitos and her husband, Darwin, made the move back to her home country. They settled on the island of Cebu – in a charming home on a cliff overlooking the ocean and nightly sunsets too spectacular to adequately capture in photographs. Their three little Yorkie dogs made the 7000-mile trip with them, and it seemed her circle was finally unbroken. Darwin painted murals for local businesses and played guitar at small cafes. Home again, Mitos worked her magic online, helping businesses in faraway places and writing a memoir of her life under the thumb of the Marcos regime.

But on December 26, 2021, the island was blasted by a force of nature more powerful than politics and less discriminating than a dictator. Typhoon Rai (Odette) hit the country's archipelago of thousands of islands, and Cebu was in the bullseye. The power of the wind was nearly incomprehensible. Protecting their treasured dogs, Mitos and Darwin tried at first to tough it out and remained inside their well-built cottage on the cliff. Here is how Mitos remembered the experience in her recent blog:

"Our home was like a ship being buffeted. This went on for hours until, gradually we noticed everything was becoming eerily still. It was a thick silence that stifled every sound."

The calm was pierced by sirens that signaled evacuation, but they remained, hoping the worst was over. But Odette had other plans, and soon the next front moved in. Mitos recalls that it felt as if her home was alive and screaming. The wind blew with violent gusts up to 168 mph *"...whistling through sheet metal like the fever-*

pitched squeals of babies, or the Sirens torturing brave Ulysses while lashed to the mast of his ship."

Mitos grabbed her computer and other devices she uses in her remote work and secured them in a heavy cabinet. They closed doors and huddled together until the pitch of the storm was too great to endure. *"... we heard a terrible wrenching of metal and a huge crash in the rooms upstairs. Darwin went to check it out. He gingerly went up the wet stairs and said he could barely open the door to the rooms because of the force of the wind."* Coming back down the stairs, Darwin shouted, *"Our roof just blew away!"*

They quickly moved to a small laundry room for safety, cuddling the tiny dogs in their arms. *"I felt like we were cast in the epic disaster film called 'Twister' and wished in my heart that this was really just a bad dream. Still hugging my puppies tightly, feeling their heartbeats in sync with mine, I blurted out to Darwin, 'I just hope that if we die tonight, someone will take good care of them.'"*

They sheltered together, and Mitos thought that there, at that moment and in that place, she had all she needed, except for her daughter, Tifani, who was half a world away in Munich, Germany. *"I struggled hard to contain my tears and regret. The moment was as cutting as a knife. Tifani's face was so vivid in my mind, and I thought, Will I ever see you again? I whispered ... 'I am so sorry. Believe me; I was not planning on dying today."*

After Odette had done her damage, they cautiously went outdoors. *"I could see that all the local fishermen's boats were wreckage or disappeared entirely. Almost immediately, people started coming over. Everyone was worried about us because the destruction to our house was so obvious and was visible from both land and sea."*

After more than a month, some electricity and water service were restored. Knowing their rental home in Cebu was beyond repair, Mitos, Darwin, and the pups found a basic rental on a nearby island. With a roof over their heads, they busy themselves with bare survival and helping others who also continue to struggle. There is little hope for rapid recovery in a country that survives on tourist dollars – now on indefinite hold.

And though they've landed on their feet (and paws), every day remains a challenge. Their family savings were swept away by the storm. For Mitos, whose work-life is online, earning a meager living remains a challenge with badly damaged communication systems.

So, if you've got a few dollars to spare, Mitos has set up a personal fund to help her family and her neighbors. The biggest problem is all the roofs that were ripped off in the storm. "I've been providing tarps for a temporary solution," she says," and helping support a dog shelter with more than 40 dogs that was seriously damaged and needs rebuilding." Never mind that her dream of returning to the homeland of her heart now lies in rubble and ruins.

It's stories like this one, my friends, that can put our own trials in perspective.

Hey, How About a Walk!

About a week ago, Murphy (my Aussie-Schnauzer best friend) and I were off on our morning walk through the winding roads of our mountain neighborhood. It's visual, auditory, physical, and often inspirational. So, I made some notes, hoping that I might be able to recreate our daily stroll and take you along with us.

It's quiet at seven in the morning in our small community of homes set far enough apart for privacy but close enough for neighbors to bond with a commitment to a rural lifestyle. Our house is on a corner – across the street from an empty lot that an eccentric woman from California's coast keeps decorated with NO TRESPASSING signs pinned to cedar trees until time, weather, and trespassers remove them. About a block down a hill is a footpath through a thick pine forest that leads to a gleaming lake – but requires a steep climb home. So Murphy and I wander up the street to walk a loop of about two miles, gently uphill, and then back down to home. Since it's early, I'm confident we won't meet with any traffic.

Cars are parked near homes designed for mountain living – steep roofs for snow, big windows and yards hosting tools and equipment like snowblowers, small tractors, wood splitters, and trailers for hauling brush and downed limbs. Neatly stacked wood piles wait for winter. Pickup trucks, camping trailers, and boats are ready for a long summer.

We turn right, up the loop that leads us past familiar homes, each reflecting owners who sacrifice the amusements of the city in favor of Mother Nature's simple offerings. Ponderosa, cedars, and fir trees stand tall like sentinels, protecting homes and hosting birds with morning songs as background for our daily walk.

I occasionally try to make conversation with a couple of species – loudly mocking their calls with my own whistle. There is one small bird that, I swear, answers me. Crows and ravens boldly fly close overhead, cutting through the air with an audible whisper of wings. They land on power lines high overhead, watch us, and shout out garbled 'Caws.' I answer them, hoping no humans are listening.

It's early summer, and wildflowers bloom like colorful blankets hugging the road. No one manages these seasonal gardens. They're random gifts of passing time that make our route a changing tapestry of colors. Up here, Mother Nature favors purple, gold, and crimson flowers, all wrapped in lush green leaves. The sky is blue with a satin luster, and the early morning sun sends bright flashes of light through blue-green branches, reaching up to where heaven ought to be. The air, clean and cool like a drink from a mountain stream.

On occasion, we meet other neighbors. There's a young man who often walks the circle accompanied by his shepherd dog, who's followed by his lanky black cat. The cat keeps pace, meanders just a bit off the path, but always returns home with them. We exchange friendly greetings, and I reign in my little Murphy, who would like to get more personal with the cat.

Occasionally, neighbors stop and chat with us as if we're old friends, though we've never actually met. We stand in the middle of the road and exchange stories as if we've known each other for years. Because living up here means we share something in common – like the brutal winter that's just passed, or the ever-present threat of wildfires over the summer, or irritation at drivers who go too darn fast through our neighborhoods. (This criticism is usually leveled at the 'elite' folks who own homes in a nearby gated community, mistaking our street for their long, personal driveway).

Murphy and I don't talk as we round another bend and trudge up the steepest part of our walk. At the top of the hill, we check out a corner house that's uncharacteristic up here. A few vehicles not in running condition, kids play equipment in various states of broken, heaps of wood and materials from some project - either planned or abandoned - and old tires piled in a heap.

We head downhill, thrilled to see the log truck parked at home and not yet on a run to haul and deliver trees from the fierce fire that, a couple of years ago, forced our community to evacuate. The family name is proudly displayed on the door of the massive cab – Musholt Trucking. The young father who commands this rig up and down the mountains is a second-generation rig driver. He's proud of his profession – one that's threatened by time and change. Each weekend, he cleans and polishes the massive cab that's the color of marigolds. It gleams like a piece of silver and gold jewelry. He tells me he'll be kept busy for a long time, hauling logs salvage from the fire that swept over 346 square miles of our county. So he drives loaded with blackened, full-length logs piled on two linked trailers from our mountains to mills in Northern California. He complains about new trucking laws and environmental changes being demanded by state regulators. Changes that threaten family tradition and an honored way of life.

Murphy likes this section of our walk because just beyond the grand golden truck is a fine two-story, elegant brick home with a lawn of green grass (a rarity up here). But Murphy is more interested in the four-legged boarders on this property. It's owned by a retired couple – a former grocer and his wife, once a school teacher who's made it her mission to rescue stray cats. Of course, it's the sight of those cats crossing the street to dine at the couples' backyard hostel that excites Murphy. The population of cats varies according to season, but it's never less than ten and often many more. Murphy loves them all equally.

We pass several vacation properties – much grander than our occupied homes. They sit silently empty under towering pines, curtains drawn. I wonder if a house can get lonely.

We're getting close to home, and we see a neighbor approaching with her exceptional dog. He's an Alaskan Husky - huge, gentle, enthusiastic, and beautiful. The dog's 'mom'' tries to control him, but he weighs more than her and has the strength of a bull. She grasps his leash and stumbles after him. He's interested in Murphy and genuinely likes small dogs. Murphy, on the other hand, is ready to charge. I pick him up and apologize for his bad judgment.

Exactly one house away from ours, I drop the leash and let Murphy race to our front door, a black and white blur of fur dashing for his breakfast kibble. At the door, I stop and wave toward the empty street, though I know you've been with us the entire journey. We thank you for your company.

Simple Moments of Calm
Amid the Storm

As if there was not enough bad news in our world, a small school in Uvalde, Texas, stabbed us in the heart and sent us into incomprehensible grief. Once again, we feel helpless to help – another inhumanity to remind us of how big and bad our world can be. It's a lot. And it can feel like too much.

As individuals, it's easy and natural to become overwhelmed and lose perspective. After all, we don't have the power to impact events far beyond our scope of influence. Alone, we can feel defeated and without hope. And yes, Uvalde left me feeling that way.

At the same time, we know that our power to help others and create change rests on helping ourselves to rise above despair. From a perspective of helpless grief – we can't possibly uplift others. So, I'm recalling a few simple moments that brightened my days and my perspective:

Fluff, Feathers, Flight: A couple of months ago, I watched out my kitchen window as a pair of Stellar Jays carried twigs and bits of string to the top of a downspout under the eave of my roof. The results were an architectural and artistic triumph – a cozy nest protected from rain and wind. I waited with them and watched as they flew in and out, each taking a turn at nest sitting. One day, when mom had flown from the nest, I stood at the window and watched – eventually rewarded with a glimpse of a tiny beak poking out from the careful chaos of the nest. I was thrilled with each sighting and discovered two tiny Jays. I worried when the weather turned cold or it rained – as if I could do anything to make it safe for them. And because they were perfectly designed by Mother Nature, the babies survived the weather challenges and soon were standing on spindly legs and thrusting out tiny wings with dreams of flight. (I worried they might fall and put a mound of blankets on the ground beneath the nest.) Then, one day, the nest was empty; no baby birds were on my safety net - and I felt oddly proud. To add to my misplaced maternal joy, the little ones remained near home, and I now spot them at my feeders almost daily – their top knots bobbing and feathers shimmering bright, lapis blue in the sun.

Wild, Wonderful: Our kitchen window looks out on a quiet road and a vacant half-acre of cedar and pine trees. It's where a community of fat squirrels live when they're not digging for peanuts they buried in my yard last winter. I've got feeders set up for them and for the wild birds we watch as the seasons change. I know that we get other visitors who come under the cover of night to eat fruit I leave on a stump in the yard. We also have fox, bear, and mountain lions haunting our neighborhood – seldom seen and always respected. But last week we had a special visit in the bright light of morning. A healthy doe wandered out from the trees and onto my wildlife buffet. My husband and I froze in the window and watched her – wary but determined – eat the pieces of apple and carrots on the stump and then lap up birdseed I'd scattered on the ground. She politely stood and posed so that I could take a photo, and then sauntered off like a graceful ballerina into the woods.

Main Street: Our nearest city is Placerville (population about 10,000). It's 14 miles down the mountain from our home. It's where we go to dine out or experience the calm and quaint offerings of a city that's not too small or so big it makes me want to run back up the hill. Placerville is steeped in Western history – Native Americans, cowboys, loggers, the Pony Express. It's also a magnet for interesting people and practices. There's a hardware store that never fully stepped out of the 1800s. Uneven wood floors, shelves, tables, and showcases that speak to its roots that were planted in 1856. It's packed with items for country living – from tools to housewares. The aisles are narrow, a labyrinth of delights for tourists and a resource for locals. It's a landmark on a main street lined with landmarks – storied watering holes – like the Liar's Bench – and cafés inside century-old shops offering nouvelle cuisine, cheese and wine shops, art galleries, embroidery, knitting, and old-fashioned candy shops. Along with its historic tradition is an unusual practice that seems to have sprung spontaneously from the roots of the city. Cars necessarily drive slowly along the narrow two-lane street. But if a pedestrian even looks as if he or she wants to cross the street, all traffic halts. It doesn't matter where – at a corner, in the middle of the block. Drivers see a pedestrian, put on the brakes, smile, and wave the walker across the street. There are no signs prompting drivers to give way to pedestrians, and I cannot find any city ordinance. It's simply a home-grown practice adopted by locals and visitors alike – a kindness that's become tradition in a little city founded on tradition.

I'm offering these modest examples of places where I find peace and delight in the midst of soul-crushing news that's delivered daily. I think it's important that we allow ourselves to acknowledge the everyday, simple gifts at our fingertips. Small experiences that are readily available and free for us to enjoy. It's easy and natural for compassionate people to feel the pain of others. That empathy is what keeps us human and gives us power to help when we can. But often, we are unable to make things right. Events are too distant, too massive, impossible to affect as caring individuals. Making a conscious effort to visit places of pleasure and positive feelings heals us handle the challenges of being human.

I found a pretty cool resource to help 'unhook' from the pressures of too much, too often bad news. The World Health Organization created an illustrated booklet on the topic and made it available in scores of languages. It's free to download (I did), and it just might help someone.

Balancing Bounty and Risk

The Sequoia Grove reigned over the land when California's first horticulturists gathered food and medicinal plants. Indigenous people were then the caretakers of forestlands, wetlands, and grasslands. There is no evidence of mega wildfires under their stewardship because, using available technology and innate knowledge of the natural world that sustained them, they became the state's first fire managers. Low-intensity fires that happen naturally were seasonal events, and Native People understood low burns would clean the forest floor and revitalize the earth for the growing season. Some of California's first people even created controlled fires toward this goal. Catastrophic fires were not an annual event, as they became under our Smokey-the-Bear fire suppression approach.

I remember when fire in forestlands became a hot political issue – it was under the broad category of "environmentalism" that started in the 1970s and grew over decades. Young people became social icons, sitting in trees to prevent logging operations. The Sierra Club jumped on board as a well-funded political force. The logging industry was decimated, and California's forestlands grew into dense stands of kindling just waiting for a lightning strike or a tossed cigarette.

Over recent decades, forest managers have embraced a 'middle way.' The California Department of Parks and Recreation acknowledges the natural role that fire plays in California's forestlands. The intense heat of wildfires cleans debris and smaller plants from around the roots of trees, giving seeds a chance to grow throughout another season. Research and decades of fire suppression led to this educated conclusion – a reality already owned by the region's indigenous people for many centuries.

Unfortunately, it's a little too late in a state with 33 million acres of forestlands. We now must struggle to repair decades of neglect. We are surrounded by evidence of our failure to manage forests – swaths of land cloaked in deep, dry duff, dead, fallen trees waiting to spread flames.

And yes, many of us choose to live in this environment – a reality that raises calls for nature dwellers to go back to the city where they belong. Too many people living too close to fire danger, the critics claim. But we who prefer to live with and in Mother Nature are not the cause of conditions that lead to catastrophic wildfires. It's overgrown and neglected forests and untended private lands that create the perfect firestorm.

I admit, driving up the hill to our home after the evacuation lifted, I did wonder about the wisdom of reclaiming our mountain home. We all know that it's not *if* another fire will burn, but *when*. Nonetheless, it took only one night in the valley to be reassured. We'd met a friend for dinner at an outdoor restaurant. A guy with a guitar and a big speaker was crooning loudly on the patio. He never took a break. With the chatter of people and clatter of plates, it was a cacophony that defeated quiet conversation. The company and the food were, however, welcome after so much isolation.

Walking back to the parking garage, I spotted a sliver of moon in the sky – a soft pastel hue, barely noticeable. Within a half-hour, we'd turned off the freeway and up the winding two-lane road to our home. Black silhouettes of pine trees hugged the turns, and soon, we pulled into our driveway, shut off the truck lights, and stepped outside to look skyward. Enveloping quiet fell, and we were wrapped in inky darkness that slowly revealed shadows of cedar and dogwood trees. We look up at a night sky alive with bright stars and a shimmering Milky Way. The crescent moon radiated a rich amber glow. And this is why we will stay, accepting both the bounties offered by our natural environment and the risks we'll face with each dry season and angry wind.

Opposites in Harmony

Readers who have been with me for a long time will remember that I often wrote about the beautiful environment of our home in the mountains, where we were surrounded by 100-foot-tall pines and cedars. Where I could walk for two miles each morning with Murphy, my dog, and not encounter a car driving on the winding streets. We often had visitors like bears, mountain lions, and dozens of deer in our yard. And, then, this past summer, we decided to move further down the hill to a charming Old West town named Placerville so that my husband could more easily do his job centered around the State Capitol in Sacramento. Instead of driving 90-plus minutes on winding roads to his frequent meetings, he's now only faced with a 40-minute drive.

Today, I live within a block of the Gold Chain Highway, surrounded by homes from a Victorian manor to small, low-income rentals. I admit it's been a challenge to adjust, but now, after five months as a (small) city-dweller, I'm finding treasures and pleasures. Placerville is a classic town with Gold Rush and lumbering history.

Fortunately, it evolved with a sense of identity, and the downtown shopping area (within easy walking distance from our house) is largely unchanged with brick buildings and old tiled roofs, tall sash windows, and reverence for its heritage. One narrow main street runs for almost a mile through the town that's made for walking.

Murphy and I are discovering treasures that are nearly in our backyard. We step out our back door, walk down a steep hill, around a corner, and there we are. Our destination is a large 153-year-old cemetery that's directly across the street from an elegant historic mansion, the Bee-Bennett House built in 1853.

The cemetery is what first drew me. A beautiful, quiet expanse of about 5 acres laid out on gentle hills. Headstones date back to the early 19th century and honor people born as long ago as the 1700s. Dogs are welcome to roam with respectful owners, and Murphy has learned to do his 'business' before we enter the resting place of more than 6.600 people. A group of volunteers keeps the revered cemetery neat and clean, and the county maintains stewardship of the property. We are usually alone in our wandering the gentle hilly landscape since we visit in late afternoons – logging steps for exercise and honoring departed people by reading headstones and giving the departed a thought. The cemetery is never a depressing place for me. It stimulates thought, imagination, and, ironically, a connection to life.

As is the historic Mansion directly across the street where couples are married amid a traditional Victorian beauty. On weekends, cars and limousines line the street and fill the Mansion's parking lot. People dressed in finery parade up the stairs and onto the ornate front porch into lovingly preserved mid-1800s décor. More often than not, we walk past just as a newlywed couple is posing for photos that will become family treasures. The building doubles as a backdrop to treasured wedding photos - the yard a place for brides to spin while the camera captures the dance and the groom beams with happiness. Sometimes, they use the middle of the street to stage pictures – couples holding hands and running up the hill to married bliss. Once, I caught them posing in the cemetery. Respectfully providing appreciation, defiance, and contrast to the background while the shutter clicked.

And here is how – after thousands of steps and a couple hundred visits – I see both the ornate house and the simplicity of the cemetery are not only compatible but also complimentary.

I feel a sense of 'beginnings' in places that, at first impression, might appear to be opposites. Naturally, the Bee-Bennett House weddings represent a profound new start for bride and groom and their families. He, she, and they will make profound changes in their lives. After the ceremony and celebrations, nothing will be the same. They will slowly adapt and grow and evolve as a couple and as individuals. They'll forever thrive on the memory of that day inside the historic Mansion across the street from the cemetery as they become new people together.

I sense a kinship, a connection to the cemetery across the street, where thousands of the living have come to say a forever goodbye to friends, loved ones, and honored citizens. It might be said that the cemetery represents the opposite of what takes place at the Mansion. But here's the link I've made between the two landmark experiences. The most significant contrast is the feelings around each – one is joy, and the other is sorrow. Both felt profoundly, intensely, and transiently. But as human emotions, they are extreme experiences that are not common to daily life.

At the cemetery, final words were said, prayers sent out to the open sky, and tears flowed. People comforted and touched each other. They shared an intense experience that would be remembered but felt differently with the passage of time. Deep sorrow transforms into sad memory, to accepted memory.

Just as bride and groom change with wedding vows, mourners bonded to the departed step away from the ceremony, needing to adapt to life precipitated by loss rather than gain. For mourners at a funeral, loss also requires change - accepting new responsibilities, abandoning a tradition, and adopting something new to take its place – much like the promise of marriage.

In these simple ways, the Blair House and Union Cemetery share this bond. Both are agents of profound change and deep emotion. Both are a celebration – one of life that was and the other of what it will be. I think they make compatible neighbors.

HAPPENINGS

Marching for a Field of Change

In 1974, I landed a pretty sweet job in the news department of KTMS Radio in Santa Barbara. I started out by doing simple interviews with newsworthy folks and then sending them on to Associated Press feeds. For example, I had a congenial relationship with former (recalled) California Gov. Gray Davis when he was merely Gov. Jerry Brown's spokesperson. He always took my calls.

But ambition and short skirts soon got the attention of the news director, and I became an in-the-field reporter. In retrospect, I wasn't great at the job, but that didn't seem to be the point. Equipped with a remote broadcast unit that weighed at least 20 pounds and looked like an old car battery, I was sent out to the elite streets of the coastal paradise to record or live-broadcast newsworthy topics.

Not much memorable happened during my time as a roving radio reporter, with one important exception. Cesar Chavez and several hundred farmworkers and supporters spent the night near the harbor on a week-long march to bring attention to the conditions they endured as migrant laborers in California's farms and fields.

I hadn't anticipated how important the assignment would be until I arrived and saw the number of men and women who'd already walked from distant points under hot sun, skirting dangerous freeways, sleeping on the ground. I was definitely a misfit, arriving in a short skirt and wearing three-inch platform sandals, hair done up in curls, and fingernails polished. I was immediately out of place. Assuming I only spoke English, a couple of the men in appropriate clothing – sensible shoes, broad-brimmed hats, and neck scarfs uttered comments about my outfit in Spanish, repeating the word "gabacha" (unflattering slang for a white person) more than once. However, they were apologetic when they discovered I spoke adequate Spanish and had understood.

The highlight of that assignment was talking with Chavez himself - a diminutive man with mocha-tan skin and eyes that sparkled like tiny beams of sun reflecting off the ocean. Some of the interview was fed live, and the rest recorded for later broadcast. But in that conversation, as his troops rested for the next leg of their journey, I felt a pull. An urge to be more than an overdressed observer. I decided to march with them up the highway to the next spot. I bolted to a payphone on the nearby boat dock and informed the news director that someone ought to be ready to come fetch me somewhere up the road.

I threw my essential shoulder bag (holding makeup, a couple of school books, pens, hairbrush, my 35 mm camera, and other necessities) over my bare shoulder and grabbed the remote broadcast unit. With shouts of "Huelga" and "Si' Se Puede," the march headed for the freeway. At first, I chatted with marchers, who taught me some new expressions in Spanish and filled me in on their goals. I felt energetic and purposeful. For the next hour, I was educated, in-depth, on the complaints, history, treatment, and demands of farmworkers. Surrounded by men and women whose hard labor fed the state and much of the country, the reality of their lives sunk in like no classroom lecture ever could.

We were marching in twos and threes along the narrow verge, rising up a steep hill leaving the city far behind. Juggling the heavy remote unit (the bottom almost certainly made of lead) with one hand and using the attached mic in the other quickly became impractical, and I stopped recording. After about eight miles, the unit itself began to drag my body down, and I started to fall well behind the great leader of the march. One of the men who'd earlier called me a "parajo elegante" (fancy bird) pulled alongside me and took the unit from my hand, giving me a look that indicated pity. He carried it the rest of the way because, due to the hills and the sun and the pace they all were keeping, I could no longer do interviews anyway.

In another mile or so, I became painfully aware of my feet - strapped into platform sandals clearly not meant for marching of any kind. I took them off and walked barefoot on the hot, packed sand. Within the next half hour, two marchers (a man and woman) walked beside me and, without pausing, removed the bandanas they'd had around their own necks and placed them on mine. In Spanish, the woman said, "You are looking like a lobster, sister." She gently took the bag from my shoulder and put it on hers. The man chuckled. They handed me a bottle of water.

By then, I realized how unprepared I'd been for everything. For covering one of the decade's most important labor movements. For walking behind a legendary leader and alongside men and women whose experience defied understanding by those of us treated equitably in life. Of course, most obvious to all (including me) was how I'd underestimated what it would take to march many miles under the California sun. My compatriots not only conquered the physical realities, they did so while singing songs, chanting slogans, and broadcasting hope.

About 15 miles up the road, there was a small gas station where I stopped and called the station for a rescue. My new friends said a sincere goodbye and thanked me for trying. "Ella esta' muy brava, pero no muy lista," one marcher about 40 years older than me said. He was right – I had gumption but not many practical smarts. The station's intern showed up for the rescue and said, "Jeez, you look terrible. Do you need to see a doctor? Your face looks like somebody boiled you." He laughed at that. It took two days for the sunburn on my neck, face, and arms to subside and for the blisters on my feet to stop hurting.

I'm thinking about that experience now as we approach Father's Day because that's who Cesar Chavez was, the Father of this country's farmworker movement. The man who lived and breathed for acknowledgment of the people who plant, grow, and pick our food. Who demanded fair treatment and pay. Who fought for humane housing and working conditions. Who created a labor union to represent the least in America's workforce. And whose effort improved (yet didn't heal) the inequities experienced by laborers who cling to the bottom rung of America's ladder where fields and orchards lie waiting for their hands.

That march and many others, by the way, did get Gov. Brown's attention, and in 1975, he signed the California Labor Relations Act, a victory for the men and women I had the privilege of marching with, though not far-reaching enough to create the kind of change they envisioned.

A Gift that's Wrapped in You

I remember being a child in sub-zero Christmases in Minnesota – my little brother and me hiding in our bedroom while the adults – grandparents and mother – fetched 'Santa's gifts' from the attic and spread them beneath the tree. It was easy to feel excitement, gratitude – first to the Santa we once believed made a personal visit and later to adults who made our Christmas wishes come true.

Even now, as an elder, I remember those thrilling seasons of opening wrapped presents and the magic of decorated Christmas trees that lit up our lives in the cold north. And at the same time, I've found my focus shifted. This Christmas I'm thinking about different kinds of gifts we receive – ones we inherit from birth families but still have to open to fully appreciate. Let me explain.

When I was in my late 50s, I discovered a natural ability to sculpt with clay. I'd tried to paint and dabbled with other artistic endeavors but wasn't really successful or engaged in the process. But sculpting in clay and casting in bronze just lit up my life. I enjoyed my time, accepted some failures, and persevered – knowing I'd only get better. I remembered that my grandfather, who had worked for the Chicago Northwestern Railroad his entire life, would sit in his easy chair and draw little portraits for me in pencil. It wasn't a hobby or an artistic discipline for him – responsibilities in his little house prevented such self-indulgence – but he was a born artist. And I believe my own newly discovered talent was a gift from his lineage.

I broadened my thoughts about family inheritance, unraveling the thread in my own. I have a daughter with a beautiful singing voice and love of books, another who teaches art and shows her work, a son who is a master glass blower and runs a center for working artists. And looking back on my own working life, I was an actress, a vocalist, and a journalist and writer for decades. Though I never recognized those endeavors as talents or gifts, I now know they are something special that runs through my family – likely for generations.

I researched the validity of talents being passed along through generations – was it strictly practice or genetically inherited? Had I asked this question 40 years ago, there would have been no definitive answer. But today, not only has genetic science expanded its understanding of the influence of genes, that information is literally at the tip of our fingers with a good-old Google search.

Brainiac brain scientists have been delving deeply into the topic of genetics. First, to look at influences regarding heritable diseases and developing some life-saving medications and measures and then to verify if or if not, talents also reside in our genes. It turns out they do.

My kindergarten version: We all have 46 chromosomes with sections we call genes. Each has strands of genetic information that determine our features – like hair and eye color, susceptibility to certain diseases, allergies, and, yes, special abilities such as an affinity for music, or art, or sports, among other human traits.

For example, researchers have identified chromosomes (oops, another explainer – these babies are inside our cells and form our genes) that relate to musical abilities. A location (loci) on a specific gene (Chromosome 4, for those of you demanding more detail) appears to be dedicated to music – singing and music perception. Chromosome 8q gets credit for perfect pitch, 12q enables music memory, 17q provides music memory, and (get this) choir participation.

The same is true for other traits, talents, physical appearances, vulnerabilities, and strengths. Of course, just being a vessel of genes that drive the development of individuals doesn't mean they'll ever emerge or be fully realized. Practice is a necessary component in any artistic achievement – without it, the talent remains dormant. And, yes, people without the associated genes can also excel in the arts or any creative endeavor.

But, the science of genetics has expanded to the point that parents can get a genetic map of their children to help guide their education and interests. Undoubtedly, this microscopic reading of potentials may also be used for less positive motivations – a kind of science fiction mind-exploitation of evil intent (yet another human potential).

For those of us too ancient to have suspected we inherited certain abilities, well, we missed that boat. I thought my interest in the arts was no more than playing – wasting time on a rainy day. The same was true for music, with the exception of learning to play an instrument. However, being a viola player seldom leads to a paying gig – my mistake! I didn't realize that writing as a news reporter was tapping Chromosome 16q – I thought it was a low-paying, fun job. And, most importantly, I had no idea I could awaken some long-dormant ability to become a sculptor, now at age 76, wanting 20 more years to joyfully manifest a gift from my grandfather, Frank Darby.

I wonder, what about you – what's sleeping on a gene? What might you have inherited along the line of ancestors and passed to your own children? It's a joyful revelation to think most of us have talents to discover at any age.

Rising Above the Moment

It's been a tough couple of weeks along the Pacific Coast and into the High Sierra. Up here on the petticoats of Lake Tahoe, we're accustomed to getting all manner of weather – from parched fire-ready hillsides to brutal winds, rain, and snow that measure in feet instead of inches. We get to marvel at the unleashed power of Mother Nature at her best and worst. Most often, our winter is like owning a piece of property in a snow globe. Fat flakes float gently from banks of clouds, dropping enough to let us strap on a pair of snowshoes and trek streets that will remain unplowed for days – marooned on an island of quiet beauty.

Our recent round of weather delivered a different experience. We've had weeks of one storm after another, each bringing fierce rain, wind, and knee-high snow. The crowning weather-related event was the loss of power throughout our mostly-rural communities. Within an hour, our forested neighborhoods rumbled with the sound of generators – kicking in to provide light and heat for … well, no one knew how long. Trips to the grocery store just a few miles down a steep and winding road became a fool's errand. When we ran out of gas for the generator, we siphoned it from our sedan.

As a backup, I pulled out our battery-powered lamps and candles, and flashlights because a generator only lasts so long as the gas that's in it - gas that's only available down the icy road covered in snow.

I'd stacked wood around our property but discovered that Father Time had conspired with Mother Nature, and the protective covers I'd used disintegrated due to sun, rain, snow, and time. Wet logs, most cut too long to fit into our woodstove. Finally, after managing day one, we sat down to escape with a little nighttime TV via a satellite dish intended for just such emergencies (Cable TV and Internet were out). However, the dish (being a dish) was filled with snow and therefore received no signal.

Cooking had to be creative; dirty dishes awaited hot water and power, convincing our dogs it was okay to wander into the storm for their daily business failed (they're not stupid). And did I mention the mountain of snow that slid from the roof of my truck onto the front windshield and blinded me while trying to navigate the previously mentioned steep and, winding and narrow road to town?

It was not until power was restored and the snowplows hit our street that I realized I was in an uncharacteristic malaise. Days of stress and demands to be in 'survival mode' had buried my can-do optimism under a mound of snow. (Let me add here that I'm aware of way worse stressors that happen in daily life – but this was my personal moment of overload.) I was crabby and bummed.

As we walked our pups down a freshly-plowed road, I had a realization. I'd lost touch with one of my lifetime strengths – resiliency. Just the thought alone lifted my spirit. And a memory smacked me like a snowball. The first time I experienced the power of resiliency and took charge of my feelings.

I was in eighth grade. A vulnerable, risky age for a girl. For most of the year, I'd been taunted, teased, and chased by the very cool girls – a cheerleader and four other popular girls. They played tricks on me – stuffing my locker with embarrassing items and assembled a crowd (football players included) to watch me open it. I wanted nothing more than to melt into the tiled floor. I was afraid to be in school, walk home, go to gym class, or visit the restroom. One day, while hiding behind a bush while the girls gathered to walk home together, I had a revelation. It was up to me to end the torture. I gathered all my courage and visited the vice principal – lodging my complaints and demanding he meet with me and the cool girls. In the protection of the VP, I forcefully stood up to the smirking teens like a prosecuting lawyer. I pelted them with middle-school logic. I even made them laugh. It worked. I'd discovered resiliency.

Since that day, I've leveraged that trait to weather many storms. Now I wonder why this recent trial-by-weather delivered such a punch. It's not like me to fold. For clarity, here's a definition of resilience from the experts: "Resilience (or resiliency) is our ability to adapt and bounce back when things don't go as planned." And life provides us with many opportunities to practice this skill, right? Things don't go as planned. A dream didn't come true. Someone betrayed or misunderstood you. We feel bad, stuck. Overwhelmed by circular thoughts that keep replaying a hopeless situation.

So when the lightbulb finally switched on as the storm took a break, I used a tried and true technique that helps me talk to *me*! I envision another person – an imaginary friend who's bummed and stressed and sees no way out of a situation. She's wallowing in self-pity. Would I treat this friend in the same way I was treating myself? As a powerless victim of uncontrollable circumstances? No. I'd offer a new way to look at her circumstances – one that includes options and the promise of our tomorrows. Sunshine for my gloomy friend. So why did I not do that for myself? Lesson learned.

Resiliency helps us react to stressful events as a manager instead of as a victim. We acknowledge that change is an inherent part of the human condition. We don't have to be trapped in the 'now.'

Shannon Suo, MD (double-boarded in family medicine and psychiatry), suggests another approach to tapping into resilience. "Some of the best ways to fill that tank include taking time to refuel by indulging in a pleasant, pleasurable activity; maybe a daily reflection on what we're grateful for, or picturing end goal beyond the immediate crisis."

Resiliency may not mend unwelcome developments, but it does give us a lifeline to another day and time. It gives us power.

So, I apologize to Mother Nature. Blaming her for a few stressful days was unfair. It wasn't her fault – or the fault of the power company or the guy who cut my firewood too long. I had a choice about how to handle those inconvenient challenges and thankfully recalled that hour in eighth grade when I found resilience, put it in my tool kit, and pulled it out when needed most.

Resilience may not come naturally, but it can be learned and, with some practice, help us rise above the moment.

Aging Stereotypes, Please Meet Reality

Unofficially, when we reach the age of about 60, we enter a new stage of life - complete with its own set of assumptions. They involve an individual's attitude about aging and also public perception – and it's this dynamic that requires attention if we want to successfully navigate our elder years on our own terms.

When I was in my early 60s, I attended a 'Mini Med School' at the University of California, Davis, for a series of lectures covering issues that people may encounter throughout the aging process. I paid particular attention to presentations that dealt with the societal aspects of growing old and subsequently dove into the topic – to, quite honestly, be surprised and dismayed. After all, public perception not only affects our self-esteem as individuals, it can literally impact our health and longevity.

As I grew older, I noticed behaviors changing toward me. Examples include increasingly being addressed as 'Dear, Sweetie, and Hon' by cashiers (Starbucks was a prime source) and asked if I wanted the senior discount. All this based solely on the young person's assessment of my physical self. I didn't suffer this (perceived) insult quietly. I left a piece of my mind with most of the well-intended offenders, and I still have pieces left to hand out.

My negative reaction was not due to my own feelings about what it means to grow old – but because the servers, ticket takers, and cashiers made a judgment about me based solely on the young person's assessment of my physical appearance – and, from there, addressed me as if I was somehow diminished - at which point I presented many of them with the card pictured above. Those of you over the age of 65 will likely know what I'm talking about.

Now, after years of making optimistic and healthy aging a personal and professional goal, I'm encouraged by the increased interest in a topic that will eventually be important to everyone fortunate enough to experience a long life. But I'm also very concerned about the barriers we continue to face. Here's a bit of history:

In the pre-industrial world, elders held the keys to the family kingdom. They owned the land and home and were the source of livelihood for the entire family, which often included several generations. Trades, wealth, land, and futures were a legacy handed down and valued. The elder in the family retained a position of respected authority – the keeper of family memories, traditions, and culture. Once that traditional family base was disrupted by the Industrial Revolution, offering financial opportunities outside the nuclear family, the dynamic changed. Of course, much of that was beneficial for people and built our modern economies. But at the same time, the hierarchal structure of the family dramatically changed. The overall status of elders declined, and, in America, older people became increasingly irrelevant as contributors to society.

Today, the dominant perception of elders (mostly in Western cultures) is associated with decline, dependence, and disability. It's apparent in American healthcare, media, institutions, politics, and government – among other aspects of life. But there is a counter to all these perceptions – and it's called reality. A majority of Americans over 60 are well, active, and contributing to society.

Becca Levy, Ph., offers statistics and science-based observations about aging in "Breaking the Age Code," a book I've read twice (so far). If the many benefits of positive aging could overcome popular perceptions, life would be richer for us all – despite our age. It's hard to overcome messages we get from our youth-oriented culture – birthday cards joking about "It's all downhill" and media that idolizes youth and supports stereotypes of aging – slow, forgetful, broken, on-the-way-out, a burden. Levy says the truth is very different - that the aging brain develops profound abilities and offers resources not onboard in our younger years. Furthermore, Levy (and others) say that when we adopt positive beliefs about aging, both brain and body benefit. Scores of academic studies cite evidence that state of mind impacts the development of brain health and physical functioning over time. Positive attitude fosters physical and mental health at any age and is particularly evident in older people.

I won't go so far as to suggest 'ageism' is a social conspiracy. But the stereotype of aging as a decent into irrelevance and disability is supported and fostered in so many aspects of American life that it's no wonder the dangers and downsides of aging persist. And they affect nearly every aspect of older life. For example: It's not okay to make racial jokes, but jokes about elders are game; the film industry seldom features older actors in positive roles (peculiar or pitiful? Yes!); medical caregivers accept decline as inevitable in older patients – untreatable - as though age is a disease). And don't get me started on the cosmetic industry and its loaded messages to women.

There is general agreement within the community of researchers and scientists that this negative approach about growing old in America directly impacts the quality of our later years. It's no wonder so many people accept these common stereotypes coming from multiple sources.

At the same time, science is busy discovering what drives some of the infirmities of older age and how to manage or eliminate them. This is very relevant as current research indicates that an optimal (and reachable) lifespan may be about 125 years! Other studies offer evidence that belies the negative assumptions about the aging experience – with attributes such as greater wisdom, calm, self-confidence, deeper relationships, and self-respect that come with age. However, these positive details are often buried in specialized sources that don't reach the general public. Levy's book and others like it have little chance of making noise above the continuous reinforcement of stereotypes about aging.

I think my attitude about valuing elders was formed by living with my grandparents for 17 years. They were my authority figures throughout childhood, and I never questioned their stature. Didn't think of them as 'old' or incapable. I loved hearing stories about their own childhoods (one born in the Black Country of England and the other to Polish immigrants on a simple farm in the midwest). Their influence made it natural for me to later work in a convalescent home and appreciate the company of elders living out the last days of their lives. They were some of the most interesting people I met while working through college. I still remember their stories.

Now a card-carrying member of the elder generation, I'd like to help set the record straight. Advancing age is not to be feared but is an opportunity to build on a lifetime of earned experience. A time to appreciate the unique gifts we bring to the lives of people around us. A call to take charge of both our physical and our mental health. To do these things, it's critical we reject the stereotypes that stalk us. Take pride in earning the status of an Elder (not *elderly,* a descriptive label loaded with negatives).

Whatever your age, I hope you'll take a look at your own assumptions about what it means to grow old.

Oh, to Be More Like My Dog

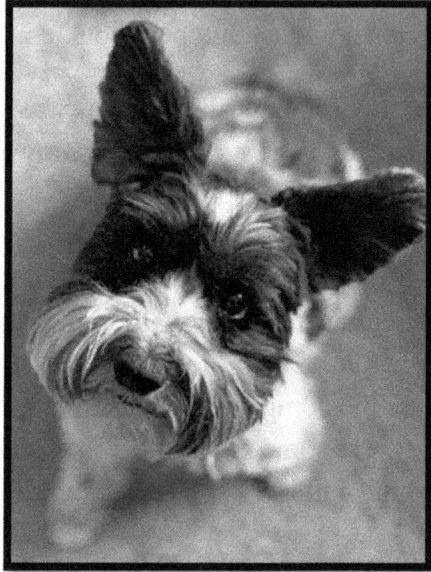

I'm sitting here with my best friend Murphy, gazing up at me from his office chair – begging for pets or treats (okay, treats). He's distracting me from today's topic – our neverending, always-available online news feeds. I'm also remembering the days when families took turns reading the daily newspaper - front page, the comic strips, sports page, and obituaries.

There was a hierarchy when it came to sharing the paper. Elders first, kids last. The sound of pages turning, the smell of newsprint, small dark smudges of ink on fingers – all part of the broadsheet experience. If you have no recollection of newspapers being tossed on your front steps by a teenage boy on a bicycle, you're likely under the age of thirty – and you missed an honored daily ritual.

The front page news featured politics, local accidents, and a bit of international news. But when we turned the pages, there was much more to be discovered. Like a clever political cartoon to be discussed and shared and a variety of popular columnists who offered advice on everything from family issues to managing money and your astrological fate for the week. Photos were mostly in stunning black and white and lacked details that would frighten or disgust gentle readers. Sunday papers brought a wealth of special items that could take hours to properly share – particularly the full page of comic strips in color. The variety of news and features mostly left us feeling informed, entertained, and pretty okay about the state of the world.

Flash forward to today. Personally, after playing a round of Words with Friends (an online version of Scrabble) with my competitive cousin in Stafford, England, I move on to my Apple and Google news feeds. There I scroll the screen for stories I feel are important to actually read and only scan the rest of the headlines. And, with very few exceptions, every item is bad news. Negative. A display of humanity's dark side. Today, those stories also offer multiple images of human foibles and suffering in brilliant color. After a half hour or so of taking in the worst aspects of life on planet Earth, yes, I feel informed and also very discouraged.

So, I'm wondering what this daily, constant dose of the dark side of being human might be doing to us. We can appreciate the breadth and depth of news now available to us, but is there a limit to how much negativity and fear we ought to absorb in a 24-hour cycle? When the absolute worst human behavior is documented and repeated from one story to the next? When there is little balance to reassure us that humankind can, indeed, be kind?

Researchers agree that overwhelming access to negative news can lead to depression, anxiety, and fear. For vulnerable people, constant exposure to violent images and personal threats implied in news stories can trigger some real mental health problems. And for those of us not at high risk – the great flood of bad news can diminish our own positive belief in the innate good of humankind.

One reason we're drawn to bad news is that we're programmed to do so. It's built-in to our survival mechanism. It's called the "negativity bias," and we are hardwired for it. After all – humans made it through 315,000 years of evolution from Australopithecus to Homo sapiens because our ancestors learned painful (often deadly) lessons from dangerous encounters with life on Earth. Forget the good times – little threat in those! But close-up experiences with tigers, poison plants, fires, pointy objects, and molten lava are embedded in the human brain. Here's how a writer for the BBC explains it:

"One potential reason the news affects us so much is the so-called "negativity bias," a well-known psychological quirk which means we pay more attention to all the worst things happening around us. It's thought to have evolved to protect us from danger and helps to explain why a person's flaws are often more noticeable than their assets; why losses weigh on us more heavily than gains, and why fear is more motivating than opportunity."

To be clear, stress and anxiety reactions are physical and observable in clinical studies of the brain. Blame the sensitive little amygdala - the nuclei in the brain that control our senses and emotional reaction to threats. The negativity bias protects us. But confronted with a daily stream of threats, what can we do to overcome or, at least, manage life – short of unplugging and camping on a beach (that's already due to be underwater in a few years due to climate change)?

Many experts suggest meditation that causes changes to the brain and helps us disconnect from irrational fears. Meditation is not an option for me – I'd have to be knocked unconscious to get into the meditative state.

I'm opting for some other suggestions – such as consciously limiting exposure to news. The American Psychological Association has a few other ideas that are within reach for most of us. Among them:

- Avoid dwelling on things we have no power to change;

- Focus on what is within our power to control;

- Do something about it – Go make a difference in a cause you care about;

- Stay physically active and socially connected;

- Recognize that news will happen with or without us – so tune out when you need to!

Being inundated with negative input throughout the day can affect us in ways we may not immediately recognize. But we do get clues when we're feeling stressed out, anxious, worried – and not really knowing why. Shut down the news feed, turn on the music, go for a walk, and try to be a whole lot more like your dog. My Mr. Murphy only wants treats, walks, pets, and love (though not always in that order). Unlike us, he's mostly in control of his environment and does things that make his tail wag. He's my role model and my antidote to online, all-the-time news.

A Few Good Teachers Pave Life's Path with Promise

COVID-19 imposed a culture of isolation on those of us who paid close attention to staying healthy and alive. Being distanced from most of what we once took for granted slowly took a toll. Friendships were different; contact with loved ones became a calculated risk, and relationships were largely restricted to a cold computer screen – no handshakes or hugs involved.

America acknowledged the serious impact of Zoom learning on school-age kids and as soon as feasible, they were back in classrooms. Unfortunately, the adaptations that kids of all ages had to make over two formative school years could have long-term and unanticipated consequences.

I thought about this while slogging through my memories of high school – teenage years in which we unconsciously choose our own paths to follow. It's when social pressures and friendships are paramount. What happens in the halls of middle schools and high schools is outside the influence or protection of parents. Teens are on their own without a guidebook and, most likely, an uncertain sense of themselves. How they navigate this intense and important culture helps determine who they become after graduation day.

Teachers in this fraught environment accept a powerful role – both as educators and as guides for the hundreds of young students who pass through their classrooms each year. That schooling has been restricted to a computer screen severely limits the ability of good teachers to guide, influence, encourage talent, and inspire individuals. Both the teacher and the student lose.

Let me be personal. I wasn't one of the girls who fit in and, in the first years of middle to high school, served as the target for bullying by the 'cool' girls and their boyfriends. The halls were dangerous for me, and the girls' lavatory was a teen nightmare. My locker became the setting of theatrical pranks, and the clique of girls and guys was the jeering audience.

And that's where teachers appeared to map a safe route to my future self. It's not that I was ever a teacher's favorite because I was an average and below student. Math, geography, history, and, God help me, Home Economics. All solid D's. So, along with feeling like gum on someone's shoe, I felt stupid. That was until I wrote an essay in an English Class taught by Mrs. Hunter (you always remember the names of the best and worst teachers). She wanted us (entrenched in a snowy Midwest winter) to write about a desert landscape. I went to the library, stared at a photo of the Sahara in *National Geographic,* and wrote. Mrs. Hunter gave me an 'A' on my essay and asked when I'd visited that desert.

Mr. Korpela, the art teacher, gave me A's on my drawings and didn't once send me to the vice-principal despite my outrageous behavior in his class. Mr. Davenport, the music instructor, made me First Chair in the viola section and didn't send me to the VP's office when I dropped an upright bass down a flight of stairs (kindling). And, similarly, the speech coach and drama coach (Mr. Stoltman and Mr. Magnussen) endured hijinx worthy of detention and still awarded me starring roles.

These people balanced out Mr. Gregory who made me sit in front of his desk, pointed a ruler at me, and said, "You, Missy, are going to be a thorn in my side for the whole quarter. I am watching you."

Now, from the distance of decades, I look back at the debt I owe those high school teachers for letting me know who I was and what I could do. And their message reached beyond my affinity for the arts – to graduating from a university with highest honors in science-based disciplines, becoming a journalist, making music, becoming a bronze sculptor, and talking with you each week.

All that – from being in the physical presence of a few teachers during the most formative years of my life. Without their acute observation and compassion, I'm afraid to imagine where I'd be today - never having believed in my own worth. That kind of influence can't happen over a screen. The culture of education is far more than assignments, facts, memorization. Face-to-face talented educators intuit more about their individual students than the kids themselves know. The best teachers throw out a lifeline to rescue kids drowning in doubt and low self-esteem.

Dr. Robert Brooks, a noted expert on education, said it like this: "Teachers should never minimize the role they play in influencing students' lives. Hopefully, that role … not only touches students' minds but also their spirits -- the way they see and feel about themselves for the rest of their lives."

It's good to know that school is back in session with dedicated teachers changing and guiding young lives above and beyond the 3 R's - building confidence and self-esteem that lasts a lifetime.

Bagpipes Play Gentle on My Mind

I did an assessment today. I have way more musical instruments than I've had husbands. That's oddly comforting. I had this thought while listening to Scottish music and realized that I do not have a set of bagpipes.

Most of the instruments I've purchased I can barely play. However, let me say that I have yet to meet one on which I cannot play *Twinkle Twinkle Little Star*. Bagpipes might be an exception.

I think my fondness for instruments has roots in my teenage years when I played the viola and oddly landed as First Chair in the high school orchestra. Viola players are rare, a bit like white squirrels. If you recall (and likely don't), a viola is larger than a violin and generally unpopular – which also describes me in high school. We were a good fit.

A viola player had more opportunities than did violinists, who had to be highly competitive for limited seats in an orchestra. There was always an empty chair for a viola player. Violin players were also pretty unpopular in cool-culture but not as unpopular as those few of us who lugged around a viola.

There were, however, a few benefits I enjoyed, like the time we went on a bus trip to play in a competition and, in the dark ride on the way home, the first cellist gave me a dry little kiss on the lips. Cellists were almost as sexy as bass players. Which brings me to another instrument.

I had a short stint as a bass player in a high school jazz quartet. Not that I could play anything beyond plucking a few strings behind the guys on the piano, drums, and saxophone. But I compensated by being cute, having a big bubble-cut blond hairdo, and wearing a pink mini skirt with white patent boots. That gig came to a crashing halt one night. I am sure you are aware that a bass is a big instrument and about as heavy as a Smart Car. As I went to return the bass I'd borrowed from the orchestra (I don't recall the permission part of that) it slipped from my grasp and catapulted down a flight of marble stairs. To call the results 'kindling' would be like calling Mt. Whitney a pile of stones.

Later in life, I occasionally played in orchestras at a few weddings and events and then eventually got a real nine-to-five job and sold my viola. But I still had the fiddling bug, and to stay in touch with strings as I traveled for my job as a magazine writer, I bought an electric fiddle. It looked very cool. And I could play it in hotel rooms using little earbuds so that only I could hear how AMAZING I was sounding. Amazing is, of course, a debatable term.

Back home, a young man who'd had too many Budweisers invited me to be a fiddler in his aspiring country-style band. All the members were at least 30 years younger than me and could actually play country music (I could not). We rehearsed early evenings in a member's garage: electric guitars and drums and me. I felt overwhelmed because I was. I had zero idea what I was doing, and unlike my bass days, I wasn't even decorative. The day came when the guitarist announced we'd landed a gig at a bar in Nevada. Instead of being thrilled, I immediately felt tired. Me – who goes to bed and reads National Geo at 9 p.m. - playing in a dive bar with beer and dudes until a 1 a.m. closing time and then sleeping in a cheap motel room? In the desert? I looked around for the nearest wheelchair and rolled out. Next step, sell the electric fiddle.

Thus it is that I came to my collection of instruments. Collecting being less challenging and demanding than actually playing. Though I do intend to (someday) play every one of them. Perhaps at my memorial service. To date, I have three violins, two guitars, a Bodhran, 2 Irish flutes, a concertina, an accordion, an Erhu, a Ukelin, a few South American clay flutes, a WWI bugle, two harmonicas, and a Stellar Accordion. I had a piano but gave it to my grandkids. After all, enough is enough. Except for maybe the bagpipes.

Flying High to a Hard Landing

Owning a newspaper with a skimpy budget and few people besides yourself to fill the pages with on-deadline content requires wearing many hats. The one that fit me best was 'ace (make that only) reporter,' though I also did graphic design, sold advertising space, and cleaned the toilet. Like the publisher in my mystery novel, *The Song of Jackass Creek*, I interacted with the spectrum of people who lived just outside Yosemite National Park in the 1980s. One of the area residents was a hot air balloon pilot, opening the door for my opportunity to take part in an annual hot air balloon race without any relevant experience, wings, or a parachute. But anything for a story.

It started in Porterville, a small valley town just north of Bakersfield, on a warm and windy summer dawn. Leagues of rainbow-colored nylon balloons were festooned across a grassy field with their wicker baskets and tanks of liquid propane waiting to take flight. My pilot was well-experienced; eager to share his enthusiasm and knowledge with this reporter. I got a basic briefing as the ground crew readied the craft for liftoff. There would be three of us in the basket – also called a gondola.

Teams hovered around their separate work areas. A giant fan filled the envelope (aka balloon), and when it inflated, one of the ground crew blasted the air with heat from the burner. The hot air lifted the balloon to its classic upright position as ropes attached to stakes in the ground kept it earth-bound. We climbed aboard – the pilot, his mate, and me with my heavy bag of cameras and cassette tape recorder. The starting gun sounded, and the ground crew undid the ropes. We started to gently rise into the air along with more than a dozen other beautiful balloons, gracefully spreading out across the central California sky.

Just as I was soaking in the peace of the ascent, the pilot pulled the chain on the burner to urge the balloon to rise higher, faster. It was a full-on shrill scream from a mini-blast furnace that caught me by surprise and made the pilot laugh. "Yeah, people think this is a quiet, easy ride," he said. "Nope. Not."

Balloons generally go with the wind, and I was confused about how anyone could actually 'race' and head toward a destination. The best pilots assess the wind speeds and direction at various altitudes and try to catch the ones best suited to get them where they intend to go – rather like a surfer catching a wave, except you can't fall off the balloon and swim to shore.

In between blasts from the burner, it was, indeed, peaceful and, due to the high level of risk involved, also terrifying and exhilarating. People and cars were ant-sized, hills looked like folded cake batter, and the fields were quilts of gold and green. I took lots of photos and chatted with the pilot. We were so deep into our conversation that he seemed to have lost interest in the racing part of the event. In fact, so excited about explaining the nuances, thrills, history, and dangers of ballooning that he failed to notice we'd dropped significantly in altitude. It was a shout from his mate on the craft of "SHIT!" and urgent use of the burner that brought our attention to the power lines directly in our path. One of the "dangers" my pilot had just described.

Since I am writing this now, you can rightly assume that we missed the electrifying death trap. By mere inches, in fact. We mutually decided that landing the craft was likely our best option since we'd also lost sight of the other balloons, and this reporter was stifling desperate screams. We rose mere inches to clear the lines, caught a breeze, and glided over a field of corn that had been cut down and bleached almost white by the sun. Ragged stalks stood upright like little swords, and there was no flat, cushy place to land the craft that was still speeding forth in horizontal flight. As we continued to lose altitude, the field became a blur, and the pilot shouted, "Down!" We crouched and almost immediately crashed into the dying field of corn. The stalks cracked and popped like fireworks under us. Finally, the basket violently tipped on its side and dumped us all out. We tumbled across the ragged bed, feeling tiny piercings from the spent crop. I rolled to a stop, still clutching my Minolta (I had priorities), and looked for my team. Slowly, each of my mates sat up and looked around, dazed but mostly unharmed. The basket and balloon, alas, fared worse.

Our unplanned landing had been monitored by another balloonist who radioed to get help for the idiots in the cornfield. I could see him hovering above, waving and laughing.

Satisfied to be alive and still in possession of my camera with its roll of black and white film, I counted the assignment as a success, even though my buddy, who owned the aircraft, appeared close to tears. Deflated, much like his rainbow-hued balloon spread flat upon last season's crop of corn.

Hands-on Heads up Parenting

I have the pleasure of living across the road from an exceptional family. Mom, Nic, is a hospice social worker; Dad, D, is a Pilot (among many other things), and their two sons, who I've watched growing up through their teen years. Yup, those years when kids are rebellious and experimenting, finding trouble – both good and bad.

Now they are 16 and 17 years old. They launched a modest handy-person business for the summer months (parents insisted they be busy during vacation months), and the boys are booked weeks in advance. The teenagers are smart, caring, polite, and respectful. They do well in school, love being out in nature, and both play music - one on drums and the other on electric guitar.

This year, they both achieved shared goals through saving their money by making and selling holiday candles and raking messy yards (including mine). After years of saving, they both purchased their first cars – two old VW Beetles. One boy earned his driver's license, and the other his permit. Neither car was in running order. They've spent many months working side by side with their dad – a guy who can fix, do, and build almost anything. The boys now know their Bugs from the inside out. I cannot picture a day when they will not respect their cars or the rules of the road.

The family does almost everything together. They camp in the mountains and swim in pristine lakes. They make annual trips to landmark places like Magic Mountain, where they all love the most terrifying rides, and to the shores of the Pacific to wander a beach they've been visiting since Mom and Dad put their parenting plan into action.

That plan has played out against many odds – the era in which teenage boys often bow to temptation and through extraordinary pandemic isolation and separation from their friends. All this while experiencing the normal rebellious urges of morphing from childhood to adolescence.

But that was by design – a plan developed by two people whose own childhood conjures up hurt and regrets - parenting that lacked the consciousness my neighbors now shower on their boys. The scars of childhood haven't healed for Nick and D, but they were motivated to plan their own path to healthy parenting. I've been watching it play out for about six years, and I know they're doing something absolutely right. I want to share a few of their strategies with you.

Mom tells it best – her reflections on bringing up great boys require no editing or comment from me:

"It's not simple. It's messy. They haven't given us a run for our money yet with the teenage rebellion. Not like I did with my parents. I was hell on wheels."

Nick credits her husband for his inner patience and open mind. "And if I'm being really honest, I would say that D spends a lot of time really trying to understand how they feel and what they want… Like he's more patient with that than I am. And because of that, when they do want something that might not be our first choice for them, we've had many calm discussions about it, and D has been able to really understand their point of view … It makes it hard for me not to see it and respect it too. Even if it's not something I want for them - like getting an Xbox, for example. They talked a lot about it, and it really was important to the boys. And D helped me see that it probably wouldn't be the end of the world if they got one."... with limits, Nick added.

But screen time was never a competitor for their sons' attention. "We limited technology. Nobody used a computer until they were in, like, fifth grade. Nobody had video games until they were in high school ... I think a lot of teens are not coping well because they live in a digital world, and they don't know how to navigate through tough situations. So, their anxiety and depression is through the roof, and everybody's off the rails."

"We do things differently than other families do. We make them have real conversations with people, we hold them accountable for their behavior ... We don't shelter them from the work that it takes to navigate dealing with people." This is a daily lesson - now that the pair have been working on their own – making appointments and negotiating business. Nick says they argue daily about who did or didn't do what. But they're solving the conflicts on their own, learning real-life lessons.

"Part of it is, I think, that we just got really lucky because both boys are a lot more like D than they are like me, temperament-wise... But I also believe that we are navigating these uncharted waters smoothly, in part because we have fair winds and calm seas, and in part, because we spend so much time with them, doing things together, and learning who they are."

"Being a mom has been the biggest, best, most amazing, and rewarding experience of my life. "If I were telling others how I felt about the best way to raise kids, I would say 'raise them like they are the most important job you'll ever have. Because they are.' And I would say, 'don't f*** up.' And when you do (because you will), tell them you're sorry right away. Even if they've made you stinky mad."

"And my husband would tell you that if he can't think of a good reason to tell them 'No,' he's going to say 'Yes'... And I learned that that's really good for kids. He taught me to say 'Yes' to them more.

I tell Nick (a passionate, expressive writer) that she owes the world a book about heartfelt, hands-on parenting in the digital age. But she's too busy living the plot.

Slithering up to a Lifetime Fear

I don't have a lot of unreasonable fears. Only two come readily to mind – needles and snakes. The first comes from a childhood experience with hospitals – indelibly imprinted on my brain. The other comes from my youth when I was chased by a neighbor boy who liked to fling garter snakes at me throughout summer vacation (He grew up to become a psychiatrist). Thus, when it came to my attention that a local rattlesnake hunter named Leroy would make an interesting story for my mountain paper, I decided to 'grow up' and 'get over it.'

The road to his home was steep and winding, lined with gnarled manzanita. It led to a three-story house that had the look of an owner-built home, maybe not totally up to code. But few folks in that niche of the Sierra cared about regulations they regarded as nobody's business but their own.

As I pulled into his driveway, an eager Australian Shepherd bolted up and barked greetings, followed by Leroy and his wife, a wisp of a woman made even smaller because of Leroy's girth and height. They were all smiles. Even the Aussie was showing his teeth. We said our hellos and headed for the house. I kept an eye out for any suspicious slithering in the bushes.

The living room was all flowered upholstery and filmy curtains, country cute. I took a spot on the well-loved couch. Leroy occupied the Naugahyde lounger and enthusiastically launched into an explanation of the attraction, thrills, and perils of rattlesnake hunting. The side table next to his chair held the object of his fascination – a taxidermied rattler, classically coiled, head up, mouth open and forked, red tongue protruding between two yellowish fangs. It was proudly ensconced in a glass dome. He also had a box that held dozens of tiny bones. He handed me a few and proceeded to educate me about rattlesnake behavior – as though there actually was a standard for that.

Leroy told me that he'd love to take me outdoors and "show me how it's done," but I wasn't (thank heavens) wearing the right outfit for a hunt. He explained a hunter needed high boots, a pair of chaps, a forked walking stick to poke things, and a pair of six-foot snake tongs. He pointed to a spot on the carpet and pantomimed a catch. "See, that there is a brush pile alongside a fence. Little mice and such like to hide in there, and it's perfect for a rattler. That's his huntin' ground."

He jiggled a pretend stick at an imaginary pile with his left hand and with his right, rammed invisible snake tongs into the carpeted floor. "Git him right behind the head so's he cain't rear up and gitcha!"

Leroy flashed a wide smile just as his wife walked in. She was grinning and carrying a tray. "Whoo-ee, what do we have here," Leroy sang. "This is sumpthin' special just for you!" (Referring to me, I feared). His wife put the tray down on the coffee table. There were three forks, paper towel napkins, and a plate of what I hoped was chicken or fish, but logic told me it wasn't. "Here you go, rattlesnake steaks!" Leroy confirmed.

The wife (whose name was never shared with me) served up generous pieces of white meat surrounding a spine with bones radiating outward from the center. I lacked any reasonable way to respond and tried to place myself in a trance. A 'just do it' trance. I accepted my treat on a tiny paper plate and poked at the meat. The couple dug in, and Leroy let loose with a few grunts of satisfaction. "Now, don't you go sayin' it takes like chicken!" he joked. I agreed. It did not taste like chicken. It tasted like my worst nightmare.

The wife wore an expression of satisfaction. "Now I know you two have gotta talk, but you just take out a moment to enjoy. It's not everybody that gets to sample fresh rattler steaks," she bragged (and I did feel special). She and Leroy bit into their fillets with pride and enthusiasm. I struggled to remain calm and in denial - though this was not possible since the fried fillets looked exactly like what they were. Having forced down one portion, I told them I was grateful for the treat but that, after all, I came there to ask questions, and I was on a very tight deadline. The wife politely said she'd wrap up a couple of morsels for me to take back to the crew at the paper.

Leroy and I chatted some more about the danger and skills and rewards of being a bonified rattlesnake hunter. He told me he even considered himself an "enviro" who wasted none of Mother Nature's gifts. I dutifully scribbled in my reporter's notebook and took a few photos with my Minolta, all the while feeling uncomfortable writhings in my stomach. That done, I packed up my gear.

It took all the control I could muster to walk calmly out of the house instead of bolting to my car. I thanked Leroy and told him (in total honesty) it was an unforgettable experience. His wife dashed out, "Oh! You almost left your fillets on the table!" she chirped and handed me a wrapped package. I made it back to my little office in North Fork, acutely aware of the emotional load I was transporting on the seat next to me. Oil from frying had saturated the butcher paper, and two perfect circles sat coiled inside, waiting to strike.

But once I realized I wouldn't have to touch the package and could get the most junior member of my team to take it inside (or, better yet, to a dumpster), I adopted a positive outlook. I had the story and, with it, a memory that, unfortunately, would last a lifetime.

Going Along to Get Along

Over the past few years, I've felt myself going from baffled to shocked and now deeply concerned. I was once an involved professional engaged in reporting (among other things) government and politics. As a reporter for a largely conservative daily newspaper in California, part of my job took me to the state capitol building to keep track of who was doing what to state policies and politics. The beat required endless hours in hearing rooms and tight reporting deadlines – stories were not yet sent via that thing called the Internet. That meant taking notes and drafting some stories by hand to later enter into basic computers, then called Workstations, in the newsroom. Sometimes, I'd be relegated to sitting on a bench in a marble Capitol hallway to write my notes and start stories.

That was before one conservative Assembly member asked if I'd like to use a vacant desk in his office. I was grateful and took advantage of his offer several times – with no exchange for favorable coverage of his performance as a lawmaker. The same was true in our newsroom. I was surrounded by opinion writers and reporters who leaned to the political right. But we respected each other and went out after filing our day's stories to share a drink at a nearby watering hole.

Well, that era seems to be over. Today, folks feel free to drive sharp spikes between conservatives and liberals like they're barricaded enemies. How did that happen? Is it a natural state or manufactured by partisan plan? Turns out, it's mostly the latter.

I slogged through many neutral, trustworthy resources on the origins of the human psyche, and there's agreement that (sadly) our mental leanings toward a conservative or liberal point of view are onboard at birth. Since my sources necessitated reading dense papers with scientific terminology, I had to ask Google to translate lots of the references in the analyses. I'll spare you that by leveraging my former experience teaching English as a second language to immigrant students. Because, indeed, scientific jargon is a foreign language for most of us.

Here's an oversimplified description: The left and right amygdala are brain regions that regulate various emotions. The right portion processes emotions like fear and evaluating threats. The left side more easily accepts ambiguity – or uncertainty. Obviously, humans need both systems working to survive threats. But we're born with a dominance of one side over the other – perhaps making us lean politically right or left.

Another more easily understood explanation comes from Psychology Today – based on brain research findings and no medical-speak:

"Conservatives and liberals interact with groups and address their members' welfare differently. Conservatism is avoidance-based - focused on preventing societal losses. It accomplishes that by regulations, restrictions, and inhibitions. Liberalism is approach-based - focused on positivity and societal gains and thus regulates via interventions as opposed to tight restrictions. Furthermore, conservatives are concerned with marking clear inter-group boundaries, whereas liberals focus on intragroup variability and interdependence."

There are no moral judgments in these findings, and most of the time, Americans have been able to accept differences and overcome them through negotiation and compromise. But what I'm seeing in our current political climate is disregard for the greater good and emphasis on winning points at any cost. Divisiveness versus collaboration.

The country has exploded with hate-driven online forums. Media personalities spew ideas, opinions, and inaccuracies that serve their best interests – truth be damned. In short, there's little middle ground where people of all stripes might meet, agree to disagree, and move forward with regard for public good instead of personal interest.

We all have our biases and leanings – to the right and left. It's good to know that some of these preferences come onboard at birth – so that we understand our political and social leanings aren't just a product of considered choice. We all naturally gravitate toward that which suits our best survival instincts – driven, in part, by our brains at birth. At the same time, as big-brained beings, we have the capacity to question our assumptions and understand how someone else can hold differing opinions. This, of course, requires conscious thought and self-examination. Unfortunately, today, there's little to encourage us to take a neutral, analytical approach.

Surely, we're being offered an abundance of channels to support whatever beliefs we might have, thanks to the depth and reach of partisan platforms. Each seeks to draw our attention and support whatever biases we already have. They force us into rival camps of 'us' and 'them.' But knowing that our political leanings are malleable and open to self-examination gives us the opportunity to re-think how we express our opinions. With vitriol? Condemnation of the 'other side'? Or with polite acceptance (not necessarily approval) of opposing views.

I take clues from my own personal experience. I live in a conservative environment surrounded by folks who generally resent political liberals (that would be me). But there is an unspoken agreement that, when we interact, our relationship and dependence on each other is more important than polarizing politics. We have a lot in common. We love the rural lifestyle, enjoy Mother Nature, depend on each other for goods and services. We base our relationship on an unspoken agreement. "You're my neighbor; I respect you. And one day, we may need each other."

After all, I didn't strive to be a 'lefty,' and my neighbor didn't have to practice to be a right-winger. But we can both choose to respect our differences by calling on our better angles, who are neither red nor blue. The last time I checked with mine, she was a whispy violet. What color is yours?

Free to Give and to Receive

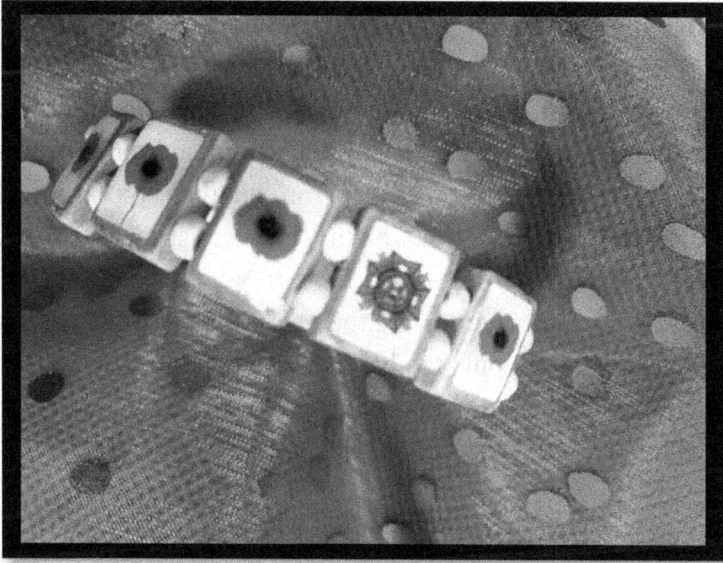

A cold November morning. I'm slogging through the parking lot of our small-town Safeway on my way to buy a few necessary items. I'm neither excited nor bummed – just doing some necessary things. At the entrance, there's a card table set up, festooned with flags and poppies, reminding me it's Veterans Day. Sitting at the table is a long and lean man with wavy white hair. He's wearing a denim jacket and vest adorned with medals and ribbons. I nod to him and smile, mentally adding some cash to my list of things needed – a small donation.

The aisles are not crowded, but still, I'm wary of being up close to other shoppers in our rural area – many have been ardent

COVID deniers who remain unvaccinated. So, my trip is swift and a little stressed. Blasting out of Safeway, I see the Vet's table and realize I forgot to get cash. I dig through my little purse and come up with one insufficient dollar. I hand it to him and figure he's likely a Vietnam Vet. My era of remembrance. And I was one of those out marching against that war. Not against the soldiers but the war. I thank him for serving and ask him if he's cold (it's freezing).

I apologize for not having more to donate to the local VFW he's representing. He leans back and smiles. He tells me that's just fine – no need. Just stopping by was enough. He offers me a traditional Veteran's Day Poppy – I thank him and tell him to save it for his cause. He picks something from another box on the table. "Here, take this," he says. It's a tiny bracelet strung with brown elastic and rectangular plastic beads of poppies and the VFW emblem. I again decline, knowing they have to pay for their trinkets. But he is adamant and puts the bracelet in my hand. I slip it on. It's lovely. I realize it's a magic bracelet because I'm no longer in neutral. Instead, I'm inspired. Grateful. Connected.

I'm wearing the bracelet as I write this. Because it's still magic. Let me explain what I mean.

Most of us go about daily life without either enthusiasm or obvious trepidation. We seldom expect surprises that disrupt predictability. But over the past couple of years, I've been a disruptor. When I interact with someone – say, placing an order or bagging groceries – any one of such common encounters – and I am able to notice something special about him or her, I say it. I intrude on our normal exchange with an unexpected, true observation.

Here are a few examples: "What pretty earrings you're wearing! …" and "What a pleasant voice you have …" and "You've been so helpful, thanks a bunch," and "Wow, you have the bluest eyes!"… and "I love how you handled that problem, nicely done…"_ and .. well, you get the picture. I intrude on the everyday moment with a positive and personal remark. And each time, I get a surprised and grateful reaction. We share an unexpected interlude that leaves us both in a better mood.

The fact that I also feel a little elevated by these exchanges made me curious. Sent me to Googlesphere where I found support for my personal goodwill mission. And, it seems I was on to a real thing. According to folks with lots of letters after their names: "Appreciation for another person lights up parts of the brain that also activate when you get a monetary reward." It's not just a flash point that lasts a couple of seconds and then vaporizes. We experience observable changes in parts of our brains tuned to react to feeling good. What's more – this happens for the giver as well as for the receiver.

Here's a science geek explanation: Under stress, bodies and brains release chemicals to handle the load – among those is cortisol. To reduce the need for cortisol, we seek out remedies such as rest, meditation, exercise, calming music. But guess what? Receiving compliments and positive feedback from other people produces the same result and with two-way benefits.

But Americans seemed trained to *not* interfere with personal space, especially with strangers. So, anxiety about violating this borderline is natural. Lots of us are afraid to intrude. However, I've learned a few things from my own experience as a serial breacher. Here are my guidelines, supported by experts on the topic.

1. The observation must be true and sincere;

2. My 'compliment' should be specific - relative to something I can observe

3. The comment will be short – not one to open a discussion but simply to elicit a positive reaction;

4. My intent must be to make the receiver's day a little better.

My thinking? Who doesn't like to be noticed and appreciated? Most of us don't get enough of this in the course of a normal day.

So, as we launch into holiday mode (with its attendant stress), I'm suggesting that part of our "gifting plans" include a conscious effort to uplift a stranger with a compliment. Grocery store, gas station, waiting in line, restaurant – the field is vast and varied. To honor a stranger with just a few words is a personal power that costs us nothing and delivers many returns.

That's what the decorated veteran did for me – within minutes. And that was before he gave me the plastic poppy bracelet I'm still wearing with gratitude. Your turn next. Give the gift that's free. One size fits all!

Out of Body and On My Mind

I've had a trying couple of weeks. Our elder dog morphs from bouncing like a pup to limping and sleeping. I check her breathing frequently. Her health, along with Ukraine and the pandemic that's become endemic – well, I've been feeling an overload of Doom.

As an antidote, I forced myself to remember experiences that brought the opposite extreme into consciousness. And I came up with a memory that is even lighter than air. I want to share that with you today – in fact, leveraging your attention for my own selfish purpose. I hope you don't mind.

My joy throughout high school was drama and music – two subjects I could not possibly fail. I carried those loves with me as I became a young woman and began to think seriously about a life in the theatre. It's my grand finale from the stage, at age 29, that came immediately to mind as I was seeking escape from the weight of my world today.

I was at a repertory theatre in Santa Barbara and had just landed the prime role of Sally Bowles in "Cabaret" - Liza Minnelli's role in the movie version. I was dancing on top of the world. I had a private dressing room, stagehands who flew to the curtains to help me change costumes (I wore a short, silver lame' jacket with black fishnet hose and high heels), a professional photographer for publicity shoots, and even an understudy. We played to full-house audiences for successive weekends.

To support my stage life, I worked at a family restaurant named Mr. Frimples – where the owner took a shine to my acting talent and endured my lack of people skills as a waitress. He even understood when I threw butter through the pass-through window at the cook who'd dared to call me "sweetie." He kindly made me a hostess rather than firing me. I lived in a tiny apartment with no furniture and only a mattress on the floor – because who needs a couch when you have the stage?

Rehearsals were several nights a week. My understudy followed me like a stalker, hoping I'd literally trip up and give her the break she felt she deserved. We opened to rave reviews, and I relished the comparison of my performance to that of the accomplished Liza Minnelli in the film version of "Cabaret."

But despite the accolades, I was essentially an insecure young woman with low self-esteem from Minnesota – a farming state with scant cultural cachet. Rather than embracing the high praise about my "clear as a bell" singing voice that I got from one reviewer, the words of another critic stuck like superglue. "Ms. Patterson," he wrote, "unfortunately simply mimicked the gestures of Minnelli throughout the performance." Though I knew I'd never seen the movie version (I couldn't afford a movie ticket back then), his words cycled through my brain like a mantra. I felt panned and fried by the critic.

Until one glorious night near the end of the run. It happened as I was singing the show's title song, "Cabaret." The curtains were drawn behind me, and I strode across the stage apron wearing a slinky, pink satin gown provocatively slit to the waist. Rhinestone bracelets glittered on my arms as I moved with the spotlight, reaching out to the audience, inviting them into the bittersweet world of love and war. And in those moments, I was completely Sally Bowles - conflicted, passionate, afraid. Singing about wild nights and parties as the world approached its darkest hours and Nazis marched the streets. But Sally and I forged ahead, wiping tears from our painted cheeks and defying fate.

We ended center stage, encircled by the single halo of light. We sang:

"Start by admitting from cradle to tomb,

It isn't that long a stay. Life is a Cabaret, old chum,

Only a Cabaret, old chum .... And I love a Cabaret."

We stood with arms upstretched to the heavens. For precious moments the audience was breathlessly still. And I felt us – Sally and me - rise from the ground and hover above the stage – looking out at hundreds of people frozen in time.

A thunder of applause broke the spell, and my heels once again touched the floor. I slowly lowered my arms to see a standing ovation. In the wings, enthusiastic cast members were waiting to welcome me back from the magical place I'd been.

It was an experience I will never forget and cannot explain. My body ... in the air. No longer me with feet on the floor. It's known as an out-of-body experience that can happen for a variety of reasons, according to researchers. I still cannot explain how it happened to me – no drugs, alcohol, or fantastical beliefs on board. But with the gravity of our world today, I'm deeply grateful I can revisit that moment when I was Lighter than air and lifted above it all.

A Greater Good

I wonder about human nature a lot. Six million years of evolution has done wondrous things – given us big brains with an instinct for survival at its roots. And along the journey of time, it refined certain traits to add to that primal urge, at one time making us the same, yet individual. And when we layer the input we've received from our separate cultural experiences on the road to modern us, well, we are simultaneously complicated and simple.

I want to give you an example before I dive into what's on my mind. Humankind's earliest ancestors – as far back as 2.8 million years ago – left evidence of belief and reverence for a higher power. This, I believe, is elemental to evolutionary survival. Those tribal ancestors observed life and death and, being human, needed an explanation. Wanted control over their tribe, family, and, to the extent possible, their fate. Prayer and offerings worked as currency to influences in their lives that they couldn't touch or see. Things like storms, stars, births, and death. In general, it appears spiritual practices from the time of our early ancestors proved favorably adaptive throughout our evolution. In the era of technology and AI, a majority of people on Earth continue to worship and adhere to religious beliefs, exercising deeply held connections to a benevolent higher power.

There are other beliefs we hold close, and many are related to our collective survival. To bring this idea down-home, think about things we agree to agree about. In America, we agree that speed limits on roadways are reasonable and acceptable. We also agree that violating those limits is worthy of punishment. We believe in the collective survival value of speed limits.

Other beliefs include principles that go to the American core. We have allegiance to principles that built our country (as other people do to theirs). From the earliest days of immigrant colonists, the principle of individual freedom has been a foundational belief (For colonists, if not for the indigenous people they displaced). We also hold dear the belief that people should be free to worship as they please. These principles are wrapped nicely in the phrase "liberty, life, and the pursuit of happiness."

Clearly, firearm ownership is historically embedded in our history. Before the 19th century, when this country was in the process of becoming a nation, we were overwhelmingly rural – a vast spread-out land with unknown threats from wildlife, renegades, and pushback from the Native people whose land early settlers confiscated. It was not individuals with military weapons acting out anger, grievances, and delusions, slaughtering random people in places like schools, businesses, and public venues.

The blossoming of our current gun rights began with the formation of the National Rifle Association, which has evolved from promoting opportunities for hunting, target shooting, and fighting wars. By the mid-1900s, when the NRA became a powerful political force, the mission expanded, and ownership of automatic weapons became a fundamental, protected American right (with few exceptions). Let me now add - for readers who hold this right dear – I understand and make no judgment. I am coming to my opinion based on decisions we as a country agreed on. Things like the aforementioned right to religious freedom, the right to petition and assemble, and other constitutional principles dear to the American heart.

But I'm also looking at the frightening trend in which the number of people killed in mass shootings has escalated dramatically– emphasized recently by the killing of 18 people and injury of 13 more in Lewiston, Maine. So far this year, 560 people have been killed in mass shootings. Of those, 259 were children. If the perpetrators of gun violence with automatic weapons had no access to the weapons of war, we'd be looking at far different statistics.

I think about other aspects of American life that we identify with our deep commitment to freedom. Consider our traffic laws for a moment – we agree to obey speed limits even though masses of drivers surrender the right to drive as fast as they'd like. This is in favor of safety for the greater good. We have laws regarding food safety, workplace conditions, schooling for our children, workplace safety, product safety, and other aspects of life in America that prohibit people from engaging in actions that threaten harm. We agree to sacrifice certain personal freedoms to protect the greater good. Military firearms in America seem to enjoy a special exception despite evidence of significant harm.

I wonder when and if we might rethink the perceived benefits of readily available assault gun ownership in light of the explosion of mass shootings in today's America. Would the 'greater good' be served by limiting the ownership of sophisticated weapons designed for warfare - as opposed to those for marksmanship and hunting?

Historically, when federal and state governments log significant increases in highway accidents and deaths - rules of the road are altered in favor of driver safety. There are laws against underage drinking, when and where folks can shoot off fireworks, where hazardous waste can be discarded, and other acts that some people perceive as personal rights. None of these is as dangerous and impactful as an assault weapon in the hands of an angry, unstable, suicidal individual.

So, here's what I'm saying. I'm not judging gun ownership and recreational shooting (in the past, I wasn't too bad at target shooting). Is it not possible for gun-loving Americans to relinquish the right to own high-capacity magazines and assault rifles on behalf of our shared safety? Clearly, without access to these weapons of war, the number of lives lost to mass shootings will diminish. Not for the first time - the U.S. holds a tragic record – the most mass shootings among high-income countries throughout the world. Surely, American gun enthusiasts can sacrifice a perceived freedom for public safety.

A version of the AR-15 was used to mow down 154 people just this year. If the shooters had no access to high-capacity automatic weapons, that number would have been dramatically lower. The overall numbers and aftermath of mass shootings are overwhelming.

A large-capacity magazine is typically defined as any magazine or drum that can hold more than 10 to 15 rounds of ammunition. The data shows that when assault weapons are used, 155 percent more people are shot and 47 percent killed. We can literally save lives by banning weapons of war.

Why would we not agree to do that – for our greater good?

The trip of a lifetime

Lately, there's been a flood of news about psychedelics being used for various mental health issues – mostly for depression and anxiety. I assist in creating a publication for a group of psychiatrists, so I tend to pay attention to these headlines. But I'm certainly not educated enough to make any conclusions about this rising theory of medical use of drugs that were once both 'recreational' and controversial in the decades beginning in the 1960s. Back then, hallucinogenic were associated with 'hippies' and free thinkers like Dr. Timothy Leary and author Ken Kesey. Of course, for a young adult, that made the appeal all the greater.

I'm someone who places high value on consciousness and control. However, back then, at the age of 20-something, I felt aligned with the movement that swept from the wild California coast all the way across mountains, plains, and valleys to my little comfy Midwest nest along the meandering Mississippi. And, with this personal essay, I am admitting to you, in public, that I had a memorable encounter with an unintended, wild trip that sent me far beyond the borders of my small river-front town. Let me point out before I share that journey – it was a one and only out-of-body and mind experience. One that I vividly remember and, to this day, recall with wonderment, curiosity, and gratitude. Yes – gratitude – for returning to full conscious control of mind and body after 'tripping' to another dimension and surviving to remember a valuable stop on that 'magical' journey.

For background (and an excuse), I was in one of the darkest periods of my life. Alone, very sad. Living with cruel losses and in basic survival mode. Some of the people around me were experimenting with LSD, psilocybin, and Ganja (in its many forms). I had not joined them. Until one night when my then-boyfriend fell asleep early in the evening, leaving me alone with a small plastic bag of little capsules filled with sprinkles of colored pellets. The apartment was bare. No TV, no stereo. No radio and no company – just me with my thoughts and a heart so heavy I thought it might fall to the ground. So I swallowed one pill. And, when nothing occurred, I tried another - and soon left all the weight of my young life behind.

The first impact was visual. Bursts of Kodachrome color spiraled out from a shimmering 14 Karat gold center. And the light show continued. I had zero awareness of time or place, reality, the inside or outside world. Consequently, I was not terrified (as I should have been). My first phantasm bore a resemblance to my conscious life. I'd been writing and performing puppet shows for children on a weekly basis – and, suddenly, I actually *was* the puppet - a puppet named Fickle Fox in a two-story building overlooking the River Thames (I'd never once set foot out of Minnesota in real life). I leaned my furry brown body and pointy nose out the shuttered window, wiggled my ears, and sang to the gurgling river as it wound its way beneath London Bridge – "I am a little fox I am, Fickle is my name. I am a clever fox, you know, so come and play my game." It was an amusing and pleasantly light moment on my 'trip' of a lifetime.

After more psychedelic visions of morphing shapes and colors, I found myself in Africa – a country that had no relevance in my life outside of a required high school geography class. Temporarily landing on that vast continent, I had an experience that was not, in any way, connected to my experience, interests, education, or imagination. It was, indeed, my first introduction to the cradle of human evolution. Fifty-some years later, I remember the hallucinogenic experience in detail:

I stood on the edge of the Nile River – which was not wide but narrow, winding, and swift. The fast current rushed downriver from me and wound a curve to the right. I was alone, with only the sound of the river cascading around the bend. Overhead was a sky of bright blue. The banks of the Nile were short and steep - a reddish-brown color sprouting with slender reeds of green that bowed in a wind that I could see but not feel.

Then as if lifted on the same warm breeze, I was lying upon the water, floating with the current, looking up at a brilliantly blue sky. My back felt pleasantly cool. The front of my body warmed by the sun. My arms were outstretched, and I had no fear. And then I heard a voice. It came from a distant place somewhere beyond the cloudless sky. It was a low, calm voice telling me - "You are every Black man who has ever lived." The words were drawn out, delivered like a prayer as I floated around the bend in the river winding its way to the Mediterranean Sea.

I am a fair-skinned Caucasian female. I'd never learned anything about Africa in school, had never met a Black person, and could not (at that time) find the Nile River on a world map.

From that profound, drug-induced insight, I returned to a level of consciousness and found myself trying to navigate a set of stairs that narrowed at the bottom like an endless tunnel. Indeed, someone (I do not remember who) was delivering me to the local hospital because I'd not 'come down' from my double dose of the hallucinogen.

There, a nurse wearing a surgical mask came to my bedside and explained she was inserting an IV feed to help rid my body of whatever drug I'd taken (I had no idea). I do, however, remember her blue eyes – the color of the sky in my vision. "You have the most beautiful eyes I have ever seen," I told her before drifting off to awake many hours later to conscious life.

Within a year of that drug-induced escape from reality, I moved to California for a new start. I earned degrees in archeology and anthropology and topped off my education with a further B.A. in African studies (the sole white person in the university's program). I cannot say that the once-in-a-lifetime psychedelic journey informed those academic choices. And I certainly can't opine on the value of mind-altering drugs as medicine. But after decades of pondering my experience on the Nile, I think I was handed a universal truth. We all, whatever our differences, have roots in the continent that gave birth to human evolution. Deep and under the skin, we are brothers and sisters.

Roundup to the Poppy Corral

Her name is Poppy. I only know that because she's not dead, although she made a couple of brazen attempts to meet her maker. Here's the story:

It's about 8:30 in the morning, and we've had our breakfast after walking two miles with our dogs. I'm cleaning up over the sink and looking out at a Steller Jay swipe peanuts from my favorite squirrel. I see a hummingbird at the feeder, a tangerine-spotted grosbeak on the ground, a donkey in the street. A what?

She's a hefty, shaggy grey beast and not part of my morning menagerie. I go out to the road thinking it might be a gentle, friendly donkey – like the one lowing in the stable with the Christ-child. He or she (at this point, I am unsure) will have nothing to do with me. My presence makes it dart down a private road. I hope it's returning home – I know a few folks down that elite road have horses – so, why not a donkey?

I go back to the kitchen sink, and my phone rings. It's my neighbor, Cara, telling me there's a donkey in the street in front of her house. This time, I'm getting prepared. I grab my dog's leash to use on the visitor. Cut up a Fuji apple and put it in a paper bag. I meet another neighbor, Mary, in front of my house, and we start the slow pursuit of Poppy. This time, I approach slowly from behind. She is shy, puzzled, and determined. She stays at least 10 feet away from Mary and me, moving further with every step we take. We try to entice her with soft words and my apple. Neither approach works, although I'm encouraged because she seems to like the crackling sound of the bag – just not enough to come eat an apple from my hand.

Poppy strays from the road and heads deep into yards built on the ridge of a forested little canyon that's thick with pine duff and tree limbs. Neighbors notice; some try to help. The donkey goes deeper into the woods. A woman joins us. She has special skills and an actual lariat, which she knows how to use. She also shows Mary and me how to properly herd – arms outstretched to block and guide it in a chosen direction. We all give it a try, and Poppy is briefly within reach of the rope. But one very impressive attempt at lassoing Poppy fails, sending her deeper into the woods and down the canyon. I want to keep track of where she's going, so I follow. I tell myself I'm a fit, agile 40-year-old (though 40 is actually a distant memory) and scamper down the slope and through tangles of fallen limbs.

I can see Poppy's generous hindquarters crashing through the brush, lumbering up and down hills. We're clambering below the backs of homes where a few people have come out on their decks to see what's disturbing their peace. A couple shake their fists at me and shout – probably something about calling the sheriff's department. I shout back – "Call Animal Control!" Dogs start barking at the gentle, giant beast near their homes and at the wild woman scrambling after it like a monkey. I get hold of my senses and call county animal services myself – actually, quite a feat when tracking a donkey, climbing over fallen logs, and fighting with bushes.

Poppy has no destination in mind - and perhaps no actual mind. But as a human, I'm aware that the main road up and down our mountain is not far from this neighborhood. I can hear the sound of cars racing on the blacktop. I run up the slope to a trail that leads to the busy road and march against the traffic on the narrow verge. And there, about 200 feet away, is the Poppy girl and a phalanx of approaching cars and trucks. They're seeing her and slowing down. Traffic stops in both directions, and a few folks get out to help. I show them how to make herding arms. We form a brigade and give our girl no choice but to flee back down the hill and into the brush.

I'm right behind her – and again calling Animal Services as I question my sanity. I want to report her location and also keep an eye on her. She briefly wanders through some yards and lands back on the pavement - on the road that skirts my house. I remember, then, occasionally hearing the braying of a donkey from my kitchen window. A family who owns real country animals (beyond dogs and cats) lives there – (my husband won't even let me have chickens).

More neighbors come out to help. But it's a mom and her young son who stick with the chase, and together, we open our arms and urge the lost little Poppy down the winding driveway that leads to her home. I've never been down the drive before and always wanted a peek. The home's large entrance gate is wide open. I trot behind Poppy to keep her focused on home, but it's not necessary.

She knew it when she smelled it and freely headed through the gate and into the barnyard. The mom and boy drive their truck in and join me. We see the metal gate to her pen is also open, and we form a brigade of waving humans and urge her inside. I wrap the chain back around the gate and secure it. I toss her some apple. Poppy sniffs and eats it. Home is where the hay is.

The Ancient Promise of Spring

I'm watching billowy flakes of snow dance down from a sky that yesterday was a blazing blue. Today, the cedars that surround my house in the mountains are dancing to a cold wind, and I think I may have imagined that spring had arrived. But I should have known better. You see, the dogwood trees recently sprouted delicate pink and white buds – still tightly wrapped on slim black branches. Here in the Sierra, most people know what the dogwoods know – there is always one good snow after they shoot out their first blossoms.

Despite the winter-like weather, Easter will be celebrated this weekend. It's only right we should be reminded that we'll soon be leaving the fallow winter behind to face a season of growth and renewal. We anticipate the birth of buttery-yellow, fuzzy chicks and fluffy white bunnies, flowers pushing out from slumbering beds, freckled fawns taking their first steps on spindly legs that soon will dance confidently through the forest.

Like all the critters and fauna that surround us, we respond to the cycles of nature and experience the opportunity that comes with the change of season. Humans acknowledged this relationship for eons – from well before the birth of Christianity that formalized the celebration of Easter. Other ancient groups worshiped the gods and goddesses of nature and gathered at places displaying the perfection of Spring Equinox – think Stonehenge and Mayan monuments. Observing the balance of night and day is woven through human history.

Though Easter is deeply tied to Christianity, the word itself has roots in Pagan history when the Germanic goddess Eostre was celebrated as a symbol of renewal. Somewhere around the 8th century, April was known as Ostarmanod (Easter month in the Germanic calendar). According to one scholar, she was "…divinity of the radiant dawn, of upspringing light, a spectacle that brings joy and blessing."

Ancient cultures worldwide observed the rising of the sun and moon – the time when the darkness of night was equal to the light of day. This balance was regarded as propitious – an opportunity for both nature and humankind to renew, produce bounty, sustain all of life.

Over the centuries, we've embellished the Easter season with beloved symbols - the signature rabbit first appeared in 1722 as a character in a book written by a German doctor. The Easter Hare then started hiding colored eggs outdoors for children to find, and 300 years later, we repeat the ritual.

I remember the excitement of Easter in my multi-generational Catholic family. Saturday's confession of sins and penance given, Easter Sunday's new clothes, the hats that women *had* to wear when entering the church, the solemn appearance of priests in brocade robes, altar boys dressed like penguins in black and white, kneeling for communion and feeling the 'host' slowing dissolving on my tongue.

I also remember leaving the service and promising myself I'd change my behavior – not torture my little brother. Not talk back to my mother. Tell no lies. Even then, as a child, the promise of

Easter was motivating. Christ died for our sins but returned to life as a sign of redemption. I was on board.

We'd come back to our small house, and my brother and I would hunt for eggs and hope for hollow chocolate rabbits. My mother and her mother would be busy in a cramped kitchen cooking a Midwest Easter feast and shouting out – "Don't eat any of that candy – you'll spoil your appetite! Leave your brother alone, you'll ruin your nice dress!" By dinnertime, I'd have eaten my candy, attacked my brother, and told my mother he'd started the fight – which wasn't true. So, I'd already told a lie. Essentially broke all my Easter promises within a few hours.

But as adults, Easter brings meaning beyond colored eggs and chocolate bunnies. We are conscious of a radical change in the environment, and it's a hopeful change. As animals on the planet, we share the rhythms and cycles of our calendar year. In spring, we leave the cold and darkness behind, watch trees turn from bare to bountiful. All around us, life renews and tells us that there is hope for us as well - potential.

That spring brings a positive message for the human spirit is not just a cliché. Mother Nature helps us take part in the transformation to the season of change and growth. We gain about three more hours of light that helps us produce serotonin – a feel-good mood stabilizer that allows us to do more with a better attitude. It's also the launch of renewal for the rest of the year. We're surrounded by transformation as life sprouts all around us. Green leaves burst from baren branches. Flowers bloom, babies are born. We are warmed by the sun and filled with hope.

And in case you think this effect is holiday hype – I checked, and it's not. It's documented in neuroscience, biology, psychology, and, okay, with a little Sees, Reese's, Cadbury, and Peeps thrown in to sweeten the season.

What is it you want to experience on this annual journey into the light of spring? I'm hoping to harness some optimism to create a big piece of art for the community (more to come about this), let go of Dooms Day thinking, and capture more thoughts to share with you in writing – because you help me realize how thoughtful, resilient and sweet people can be.

Free Samples – Grab Your Grateful Boost Here

I'm publishing this just two days before America's annual day of gratitude. So many of my readers from around the world responded to my request for thankfulness that I am in the unique position of receiving more good news than any one person deserves! I am excited to share this large dose of Grateful Positivity with you – before you launch into all-consuming preparations.

A word about my editing: First, I've eliminated *most* references to sentiments we all share – gratitude for family and friends (including pets). And I've delicately edited when a response was a bit long. I hope you read through these brief sentiments, and they do for you what they've done for me – affirm the presence and power of good in our lives – and how important it is to celebrate the most important things in life. In no particular order:

Peter: Thankful that I can breathe clean air. Thankful for the sunlight I can see. Thankful for this body that allows me to experience. Thankful for all the good and the seemingly bad experiences. Thankful for the kindness and friendship of so many Beings who came across my way. Thankful that I can say 'Thank You'.

Kris: I'm grateful for every extra day the good Lord gives me. And I'm grateful for the caring staff at the nursing home where I live.

Vicki: My health (I'm 75 and & never sick!)

Shannon: I am thankful for a good-paying job with excellent colleagues that allows me to provide care for people in need of services.

Steve: I'm thankful for every day I can get out of bed and enjoy these wide-open years of opportunity.

Christina: I am thankful for my family and our third grandkid - she is seven months old. I am also happy to share our feast with our fur babies (at least the turkey).

Elizabeth: My parents, my dog, Lovie. That I have a place to live - Did I mention my parents? For things unspoken. And for Grace.

Ianna: Having all my limbs and most of my body parts in decent shape. Enjoying my job - I get paid for working with clay!

Patsy: Two sisters, far apart physically, but close with weekly phone chats. As a recent card from my older sister declared, "How does anyone make it through life without a sister?" My easy-going, undemanding husband.

The travels I've done both solo and with him, cheap via housesitting. So thankful we were able to go so many places before the pandemic. Good health, and living my dream on my Caribbean island.

Geri: For decent health; friends and family who are genuinely fine people; my plants and trees, indoors and out; and music, for all it has meant and done in my life.

Kay: I am grateful that I can get up, get into my wheelchair and move around on my own (I have Cerebral Palsy).

Alonza: I'm thankful that I have not gotten COVID-19, even when exposed. For my two new grandsons, making a total of eight now. Mostly, I thank my Lord, Jesus Christ.

Tonya: Family. Friends, health, sight, hearing, music, puzzles, books.

Anita: I am grateful … that I am currently *not* working and can enjoy 'just living' and my hobbies. I am grateful for all the things we have that we may not have in the future - like good health, freedom, and relative peace.

Kathy: My kitties, my home, my husband, my health, and you. Thanks for reminding me.

Anne: I am thankful for family and friends and wonderful authors who take pity on poor people who can't afford to buy books and sometimes send one for free. I always leave a review.

Cindy: I am grateful for the Blessings God grants me daily. I am grateful for my little dog, Brody. I am grateful for my family, my health, my home and my friends.

Mitos: - I am grateful for my loving husband, our furry friends, health, and peace at home.

Beverly: I am extremely grateful for my salvation! Also, the freedom and privilege of being born and living in the United States of America.

Joanne: I am Thankful for all my children as one almost died after severe brain damage from being hit by a drunk driver. She and another child both have Type 1 diabetes. My middle child, I almost lost to suicide. I am very thankful to God they are all here with me today. I have been truly blessed.

Deb: I am thankful that three members of my friends and family had successful surgeries and are doing well.

Nancy: Family and friends, indoor plumbing and clean water, good health, the natural world, especially the Sierra and the oceans, touch and reading.

Jan: Very thankful for my little guy Dylan when he's cuddly and not biting my feet! Thankful that this Covid pandemic is easing up. Thankful for having a mortgage-free home and income to cover my expenses.

Joanie: Good Health, family and friends, shelter, dogs, nature, and science.

Patricia: Where do I start! Got through Covid. Loving husband of over 30 years, Paid off the house this year and after 2 new knees, a hip, and shoulder, I'm still mobile and active!

MariLou: Modern medicine. Chances are my husband would be having a miserable holiday -or none at all- if it weren't for modern procedures, and that our home that was spared from the Caldor fire!

Ruth: Thankful for a good rainy afternoon in Ohio. For my family and friends and my health.

Pam: I am thankful for my family, church family, friends, and all the blessings in my life. Most thankful for my relationship with God.

Ruth: I am thankful for my sweet, patient, and loving husband of 62 years, my lovely daughter who has survived breast cancer, and my rescues "Hotshot" furbaby London and grandfurbaby Brewster.

Kathleen: I am grateful for the love of my family and friends. I am grateful for the number of nonprofit agencies that are doing their best to aid individuals in their time of need.

May your Thanksgiving holiday be filled with love, companionship, and gratitude. You, dear reader, give all these things to me.

When Every Day
Was April Fool's Day

I was listening to the news on National Public Radio. In case you haven't noticed or are living on the distant Planet Bliss where there is no news, period, what gets reported as 'news' is rarely upbeat. In fact, it's consistently tragic and paints a dire picture of humanity, no matter what continent we're on.

At the same time, most of us are confronted with bad news much closer to home. Together, we contend with new virus strains, climate change, fires, hurricanes - all this along with our own personal challenges to manage.

So, over the weekend, I found myself reminiscing about brighter, lighter days in our lives. When we laughed a lot, sought out mischief, played jokes, planned pranks. Okay – most of the aforementioned happened before the age of crushing responsibility – otherwise known as adulthood. But I was one of those forever young souls whose funny bone failed to evolve until April 2019 – when the relentless and mutable Coronavirus changed life as we knew it. Now, I feel like a full-fledged, burdened adult whose face might crack if I smile too much. I channel my highly superstitious

Polish grandmother, who cautioned, "Don't laugh too much because that means you're going to cry."

But I remember the former 'me.' The one who loved to plan and pull pranks on people – pranks that sent me (probably not my targeted victims) into gales of nearly unstoppable laughter. As Mary Hopkin crooned in the 1960's – "Those were the days, my friend. Oh yes, those were the days." And to briefly relive those days, I want to share a few of my finest prankster moments with you.

1. I begin with an event that took me most of an afternoon to execute. And another in the vice principal's office as atonement. Before lunch in the high school cafeteria, I borrowed a fuzzy green beanie hat from Don Burleigh's locker. At lunch, I told him I had psychic powers and that he was going to be delivered something very special later in the day. After my small circle of friends left for class, I remained inside the cafeteria and ladled leftovers from plates into a paper bag. I then went into the girls' lavatory, ripped open a seam in Don's hat, filled it with cafeteria garbage, and stapled it shut again. Near the end of Don's civic class, taught by Mr. Wilson, who already hated me, I opened the classroom door and, much like a quarterback throwing a pass, lobbed the fuzzy football toward Don's desk, where it landed with a thud and started to leak its contents. I was in stitches. Don was stunned. Mr. Wilson was purple. I ran back to the girls' room and laughed till I cried - and had to report to the vice principal's office.

2. As a high school senior, solid member of the thespian crowd, and first chair violist in the orchestra, I helped create an unforgettable experience under the stars atop Garvin Heights, where young people went to experience puppy love (as we called it then, "necking). A friend slated to be valedictorian at our upcoming graduation

and trusted with the family sedan drove our group of five friends up the winding hill, where we parked and picked out a grey Chevy in which the windows were steaming up. With animal stealth and viola and bow in my hands, I crept up to the rear of the Chevy, gave the rest of my crew a high sign, and started to play "The Anniversary Waltz" while my friends carefully wrapped the victims' car in fathoms of toilet paper. (We'd successfully done this before, by the way). However, this young lover wasn't amused, and as we piled back in the getaway car, he chased us. Once speeding down the hill, we attracted the attention of a local police car, ended up stopped, and escorted home to parents who were not (unlike all of us except for the valedictorian) laughing.

3. Let's jump ahead by about 45 years to demonstrate how long an adult woman can desperately hang onto immaturity. My husband (who, against all odds, is still with me) was at a meeting near the State Capitol with doctors on the board of a professional medical association. Knowing that he was surrounded by high achievers and genius intellects, I felt the need to bring him home to bread and butter reality. I had a large metal and glass bird feeder that was guaranteed to be squirrel-proof. I placed it on the middle of a table on the back deck, under glowing yard lights. I borrowed my dog's favorite stuffed toy (a grey squirrel) and sat him inside. Figuring the meeting was near the end, I texted my husband with a shadowy picture of a squirrel in the squirrel-proof bird feeder. With amazement, I told him how unbelievable it was that a squirrel actually got inside! I said I was too afraid to let the poor little guy out. Husband shared this bit of news with ten brilliant physicians. Once home, husband grabbed a broom and snuck out the backdoor like a big game hunter ready to

strike. Two feet away from the feeder, it dawns on him the squirrel is not moving or even breathing. I'm crying again. He wondered aloud how to explain this to his docs.

Of course, as a serial prankster, I have many more questionable events to report. Some of them, alas, were really not funny – like when I blindfolded Jimmy Streater and cut the buttons off his new shirt. His mother did not laugh. I share these less-than-proud moments in my life to, just for this moment, remember being silly, thoughtless, and without life-and-death concerns 24 hours a day. Please do not think less of me. And if you have an exquisite prank to share – I am an email away. You'll help me to feel more normal.

Is Enough, Enough?

We're being played. Manipulated. Led by the nose like a horse to water. Dog to a bone. Cat to kibble.

We like to believe that the choice of our intake of daily news is up to us. We can scroll for particular stories of interest and be selective. Skip topics we find irrelevant and focus on outlets we deem most reliable and trustworthy. With almost unlimited access to global news sources, we literally have the world at our fingertips. But, like the fantastical land of The Wizard of Oz, where Dorothy finds herself in the company of the Scarecrow, a Cowardly Lion, and the Tin Woodsman, there is a Wizard behind the curtain.

Along with the bonanza of information provided by cyberspace (itself a mind-blowing concept some of us will never grasp), we're now treated to a cyber mind-reading editor that anticipates our intent and provides suggestions to complete our thoughts and sentences. Bots (online robots that anticipate our intent and provide suggestions faster than the humble human brain) work behind the scenes. Topping that is the newer ChatGPT that can be used to create entire documents for us – no actual human composition required. This clearly presents opportunities for fraud, cheating, and other once-purely human foibles.

Mushrooming advances in the powers of cyberspace have also been both a boom and a bane to the delivery of our everyday news. When we choose a source – be it conservative, liberal, or in-between, the items we find have been pre-selected for us – not by editors but by a lightning-fast cyber search for headlines and stories with keywords that attract traffic and clicks. And those keywords are almost always negative, scary, and/or alarming.

This is called "negativity bias" – which means we are attracted or alarmed by specific triggers – in this case, words that imply danger. Threatening words like "shooting, cancer, bomb and murder." We are much more likely to click through to these than, say, "kitten, smiles, or sunset." There is a perfectly good and traceable reason for this. Without loud alarm bells in our human brains, we'd be – extinct! Fear, flight, and fight were built into the proto-human brain 2 million years ago. Had humans evolved without a dominance of fear – well, we'd be nothing but a footnote in history. No more than a two-legged hors d'oeuvre on the Pleistocene buffet.

However, the negativity bias that was meant to protect us is now an existential threat. Research on our responses to certain words has been going on since 1967 and shows pretty consistent results. We're hard-wired for gloom and doom, and competitive online outlets know how to take advantage. For example, Facebook knows what headlines to push out. Anger emojis receive five times more 'Likes' than smiles – so the chatty platform pushes out more posts laced with scary or negative keywords than with calm, friendly, or fun terms. It's all about winning the most eyes to dominate the competitive market.

The connected online world is a relatively new technology that developed at warp speed. Competitors in the online market can hardly be blamed for grabbing the brass ring of algorithms that offer increased clicks and eyes. Unlike the less easily accessed printed newspapers and magazines, there hasn't been time to adopt many of the characteristics embraced in the world of print – where truth, accuracy, and public good played a role in decisions.

Psychological studies show that we humans have a clear bias in favor of bad news, as opposed to good news. Credit this to our ancient survival instinct. Negative encounters were a choice between life and death. Flash forward to the digital age of competing outlets. It's all about 'eyes' on the screen, and negative wins the competition without anyone dying.

And it's not just news that follows the lead. For three years, Facebook tracked 'anger' and 'like' emojis and found five times as many anger 😠 posts as 😊 's. Naturally, FaceBook pushes out what research shows engages the most interest and response. And, of course, they're in good company with thousands of competitive online news, entertainment, and social engagement providers. Among the universe of players in the field are social media sites programmed to support irrational fears, fictional beliefs, and dangerous theories – all free and easy to access.

So what's to be done?

Personal awareness of where and why we chose our online resources is a place to start. Competition for clicks is fundamental business for providers, and they'll do what's necessary to get our attention. So, it's up to us to recognize when we've had enough doom, gloom, death, despair, and fear. Catch up on the necessary. Choose to go no further down the dark rabbit holes.

It's like the Wild West out there in cyberspace. There's no reason for consumers (townspeople) to know that we're being targeted, manipulated, and put in danger by programmers (outlaws). Unlike the evolution of radio and TV, the cyber universe exploded. It invaded homes and lives with devices and options that were once unimaginable. Consequently, there's been little time to react, build standards, or even understand the inherent threats of a system that baits us to click through.

It's also up to us to make informed choices about what we access, for how long, and from what sources. And to know when enough is enough. We have a responsibility we never anticipated as so many aspects of our lives migrated online. It's up to individuals and families to be aware of dangers and threats offered by a system that's revolutionized our lives in both negative and positive ways.

It's interesting that we're traditionally protected from many of life's common risks with rules, guidelines, and laws. But the cyber universe in all its glory and shame erupted like a universal storm, took us by surprise, and now it's up to us. Of course, mental health experts are already talking about how to take control of content that's dangerous to mental health with suggestions like carefully selecting our news sources (don't engage in doomscrolling), limiting time with online news, seeking out uplifting and positive content.

Caving Into Our Primitive Side

I had an intense "need to know" moment after writing last week about our inundation of 24/7 bad news. Replies I received from readers highlighted how so many of us conscientiously seek ways to mitigate the effect our always-on news feed delivers. Some folks retreat to activities that deliver personal gratification; others step out to help someone in need or engage in positive social activities. These conscious efforts to (temporarily at least) rise above the downers of a now-typical news day are all good – and advised by mental health experts.

Still, I wondered why such continuous input can move in like an unwanted relative who won't leave your spare bedroom. And I developed my own theory. It may be, I thought, that we are hardwired for survival – it's how we made it from the caves of Olduvai to the Silicon Valley. Our earliest ancestors, 2.58 million years ago, had to recognize numerous threats and embed them in memory. The faint sound of something moving in the brush. The flapping of wings in the sky or movement in tall grasses meant Pleistocene humans were in danger from a super predator like a Crowned Hawk Eagle, or a crocodile the size of a Tuff Shed, or (my favorite nightmare) a 30-foot Madtsoiidae snake.

Constant demand to be on alert both day and night surely created a dominance of fear in the developing human brain – it's why I'm here writing what you're reading here today (thank you). Of course, I quickly discovered plenty of expansive theories about the adaptive, survival-oriented development of our early ancestors. And yes, my armchair theory is pretty right on. The fight or flight syndrome survived the eons from Homo Habilis 24 million years ago to Homo sapiens and the digital age.

This (and many other evolutionary adaptations, of course) protect us from harm – though we are generally past the era of carnivores the size of a two-bedroom house. Of course, our human environments are radically different than they were back in the days when the danger of being eaten by a Homotherium – resembling a lion whose canine teeth were seven inches long. But, somewhat ironically, while we no longer face the daily risk of being eaten alive by a critter in our neighborhood, we've got plenty of threats to trigger fear and anxiety. Fortunately, our wired information age not only delivers news that lights up our survival instincts it also offers avenues for control and escape when needed. Currently, that's almost every day for me.

Israel, Palestine, the U.S. Congress, politicians acting like grade school bullies, banned books, biased news – sadly, the list goes on. At the same time (if we seek it out), there is good news to be had, but that requires personal initiative – it's not spoon-fed to us by competing news sources. It's up to each of us to trigger the dopamine and endorphins that bring us calm and a sense of well-being. There are plenty of suggested ways to get into a positive frame of mind. The first is, of course, to limit exposure to the news.

Pick a time to get your fill and then shut it down. Avoid either starting or ending your day with a news feed. Ditch apps that deliver downers and news notifications. Don't worry – you won't miss a thing that's not available at another time. News happens (and is repeated) without our attention. Here are a few simple strategies to protect and defend a healthy state of mind.

Some call for developing practices like mindfulness, meditation, and yoga. I don't know about you, but none of these remedies work for me, although I can intellectually understand why they should – the techniques are not just mental meandering. They have verified physiological effects that can change a person's outlook. Override the fright, flight, freakout responses that took us from caves to college.

I'm more drawn to active remedies like taking long, energetic walks and saying a surprise "Good morning" to folks I don't know. Or turning on some loud music and dancing around the kitchen. Also, there's nothing that takes a person's mind off very bad human behavior than to commit some good behavior. Help a neighbor, take part in a beneficial community organization, go to the supermarket, and say something nice to three strangers. Volunteer for a cause or organization that touches your heart – doing positive is a requirement for feeling positive. Set aside time for something you enjoy – a project, a hobby, a passion, a person who always makes you feel good.

Let me add a final incentive to selective news consumption. We are being manipulated to consume bad news. None other than the big brains at the Pew Research Center reveal that "…8 out of 10 Americans get their news from a digital device." Their researcher further showed that "negative content drives engagement." And (surprise) this finding led to social media (like Facebook and others) to deliberately "promote negative news stories" that readers then share. It's all about eyes and dollars, francs, rupees, pounds, and ougiya (which, as you know, is currency in Mauritania).

132

According to millennial expert and author Dr. Goali Saedi Bocci, the impact of this planned attack on our well-being is serious and leads to "irrational patterns of thought that create a false picture of reality, potentially resulting in poor decision making, and feelings of panic and despair that can cause or worsen anxiety and depression." I don't know about you – but I resent being manipulated. Time to log out!

The Forever Art That
Stole My Heart

Outside of important humans in my life and our pair of precious pooches, there are two things that have kept me relatively sane over the pandemic past (and present) – one is the connections I've made with many of you – voices from around the world in diverse circumstances who write and share their challenges, wisdom, and comments with me. Each communication lifts me up from the latest onslaught of bad news on far too many fronts. The other preoccupation that brings me peace and pleasure is sculpting in clay that will, one day, transform into a work of art in bronze.

Humans first started to make the metal – an alloy of copper, tin, sometimes arsenic, and other minerals - in Africa and the Near East. The Bronze Age, 3300 BC to 1200 BC, was so important to cultural evolution that an entire era bears its name. The technology created a new communication tool that could be shared widely - beyond the walls of caves that bear the earliest human art. It was also used for toolmaking, weapons, worship, and trade. All this contributed to what we know as civilization – settled human groups united, sharing resources, developing economies, and defending their territories.

I spent some time pondering just why I was drawn to bronze sculpting – an art that is time-consuming, complicated, and very expensive to produce. Why don't I just take up oil painting? Other than the truth that I have little talent in that discipline, I realized there was a deeper motivation. I've always found value in the enduring past – music, art, cultures, ancestors, and human traditions. I've got degrees in archaeology, anthropology, and African Studies. I appreciate music that stands the test of time. And I have always found elders far more interesting than young people. In this context, bronze makes perfect sense.

I started dabbling with the art after doing a newspaper story on a bronze foundry (I was a writer/reporter for most of my working life). Most stories I wrote were filed away and forgotten after the deadline. But the foundry experience stuck with me. A little voice said, "You can do that!." I bought a brick of clay and started sculpting. To both my surprise and delight, the small statue I made was not terrible – though the cost of casting was terrifying. I was undeterred.

At the age of 59, I found myself fully enraptured by sculpting for bronze and choosing to ignore the cost of the process. I loved the hours spent molding and manipulating the oil-based clay (it never dries). I was fascinated by the complex process once the sculpting was done – the mold making, wax pouring and finishing, and the timeless casting into bronze at an art foundry. A foundry is a vast space filled with sounds of clanking chains, metal on metal, the hum and whir of air-powered tools – all in the hands of skilled craftsmen and women.

While I continued to work primarily as a writer, I also made sculptures as time and my bank account allowed. I sold some pieces and had the honor of having one purchased and donated to the Sacramento Zoo. It stands in front of the carousel where countless children have rubbed his head for many years, making it shine with love. A few of my works have won accolades and awards – Best in Show and Blue Ribbons.

It's been particularly gratifying to work on commissions like the image of Lucy, a beautiful Golden Retriever who went to dog heaven just months after I completed the piece. It's now installed on a lovely chest that holds her ashes and so many memories. It's a privilege and a trust to work with people to transform an idea into an everlasting artwork, a benefit I never imagined when I dove so fully into my passion for bronze sculpting.

My biggest and most challenging work is a near-life-size bust of Pope Francis that took me about two years to complete. I still ask myself, "why." His face popped into my head while I was sitting under pine trees at a picnic table in the Sierra, and I started the sculpture then and there. I admire this Pope – his compassion and kindness and ability to resist the Vatican bureaucracy. He cost me $5,000 to liberate from the foundry. He won the Blue Ribbon at an art show last year and awaits adoption by a nice Catholic parish.

And now, into what we hope are the waning months of the pandemic, I am even deeper into my obsession. With the help of a partner who knows about marketing and fundraising, I'm sculpting a monumental tribute to honor the men and women who fought to keep our homes safe from last year's Caldor Fire. I'm also working on a sculpture of the cheetahs at the Sacramento Zoo for their annual fundraiser.

I'm so grateful that sculpting kept me engaged and imagining and never bored throughout the trials of the Pandemic. My biggest regret is that I didn't discover my passion when I was far younger – I often think about how much I would have learned and improved in the art over decades of experience. Now, my best hope is to emulate Grandma Moses, who found her art very late in life but never let time defeat her passion.

Backdoor to a Writing Life

In keeping with my life as a person with too much curiosity, I chose to study archeology, anthropology, and African Studies at UC Santa Barbara. I have degrees in each. I planned for graduate school and applied to some prestigious halls of learning. At one, I met a refusal (despite graduating at the top of my class) because the quasi-famous archeology professor in charge mistook me for someone else. "Oh, so you're Miss Patterson," he said in a white South Afrikaans twang. "I thought you were some fuzzy-thinking Black woman looking for her roots." After telling the Prof what he could do with himself and his department, I decided academia was not for me.

Instead, I ran away from Santa Barbara and fled to North Fork, a small town on the petticoat fringe of Yosemite. My trip there was with a dynamic man who picked me up in a bright yellow school bus and hauled my educated self-up a mountain six hours away. North Fork took pride in claiming to be "The exact geographical center of California."

He was a house builder, an architect, a mesmerizing bolt of energy with wild eyes and the imagination of a combination Thomas Edison, Frank Lloyd Wright, and Jim Carrey – with a little Jane Mansfield thrown in. If that sounds dysfunctional and a bit crazy, it was also a wild adventure, and I married him anyway. On a random weekday, we drove by a little church tucked into the Pines and found the preacher finishing cement inside a septic tank. He crawled out, wiped his hands on stained overalls, and snapped his Stihl Saw suspenders with his thumbs. I became a Mrs. – not for the first (or last) time.

In the small town that's now at the center of my *"Song of Jackass Creek"* mystery novel, I quickly discovered that my college education was as useless as a one-legged man in a butt-kicking contest. Jobs in North Fork included waitressing and working at the sawmill. In order of the aforementioned careers – I'd been fired from food service after flipping butter through the pass-through window onto the face of the cook who'd just called me "Hon;" been ordered off the grounds of a factory when I'd removed my boots and was (justifiably) berated by the foreman who also fired me and to whom I sang, "These boots are made for walkin'," (and that's just what I did).

At the same time, the husband, whose true aberrant self emerged more every day, decided we could build an entire house in one week. It was the pinnacle of the owner-builder movement – lots of unqualified people were building structures that would not meet with county approval and were best attempted on property that was remote and nearly inaccessible. Ours was on top of a hill, overlooking the narrow road into town. Visible to all. Nonetheless, together, we built a board-on-board house that was supported by wooden piers, constructed in the shape of a rounded letter "M" so that, by virtue of its curves, was self-supporting and would not collapse. It took exactly seven days to complete.

I then addressed my lack of a job by creating one that I knew nothing about. I started a little newspaper called *The Timberline Times* – a tabloid-size paper that ran about 12 pages. At the same time, I discovered two important things – we were expecting a baby, and the husband liked to wear my underwear.

My little paper became popular, and I got to be a local celebrity. The guy who owned the gas station gave me free tankfuls so I could travel to do stories and sell ads. Advertisers felt sorry for me working "in my condition" and bought ad space. And, due to the lack of healthcare in the region, I hooked up with the local midwife.

Just before the paper was due to go to the web press in the valley, I was hunched over the old-time layout boards, pasting up stories before the days of digital publishing when the labor pains started. Stopping to breathe between the Box Feed Store ad and a story about a baby goat, I managed to get the layout done and out the door. By then, it was night. Dark descended on the mountain where streetlights were nonexistent, and all navigation was done by headlights and memory. We'd never before been on the dirt road to the midwife's home deep in the woods, and the husband barreled along, fueled by adrenalin to the sound of me moaning like a banshee. At a fork in the road, under the arbor of leaning oak trees, a red fox lept over the car's hood. I screamed, "RIGHT!" (I don't know why). And we landed at her home, where a post-Thanksgiving party was in full swing, and the waterbed was vacant. It wasn't ten minutes before the baby boy was born with one eye wide open, delivered by the veteran midwife.

We spent two days in our board-on-board house, and then the brand-new human and I were back at the newspaper office, reveling in all the attention and happiness we brought to Main Street North Fork. For the rest of the time the baby and I lived there, we traveled together to sell advertising (he was an effective motivator for merchants to say "Yes" to me). We eventually left the town, just he and I, to pursue new adventures. On the way out, I gifted his father with some of my old outfits, which I knew he'd one day appreciate.

This, my friends, was how I entered my career in journalism through the backdoor of opportunity.

Arrested Development

It's hard to believe it was just 60 years ago that I went with my friends to a popular hideaway where couples parked in cars to snuggle and smooch. There, I put my viola (the larger, deeper, and more soothing cousin of the violin) to my chin and played "The Anniversary Waltz. I'm sure a few of those young lovers still remember. Perhaps not fondly.

Having recently reconnected with a few old (I mean that literally) schoolmates back in the Midwest, I was suddenly visited by a vivid memory of how my theatrical mates and I spent some weekend nights of our senior year demonstrating our talents and immaturity.

From the distance of time, I can understand our behavior. We were high school performers – actors, orchestra and band members, stars of the Speech Club, and so full of ourselves. We bonded around competition for roles and attention and performances that somehow proved we were important. A few of us (not me) were also high academic achievers and scholarship recipients.

Living in a small city on the banks of the Mississippi, recreational activities were limited. Unless you count riding a public bus or ice skating in the gutters. As a creative clan of seniors (I mean the first time around, not our current status), it was often up to us to invent our own weekend activities. One boy had access to a family car and a driver's license (a rarity in those days). That vehicle entrusted to the son of a prominent resident was our key to nighttime adventure.

After dark, we'd drive around parking lots at Lake Winona – a puddle compared to lakes I'd later see outside our sheltered town. We'd next drive up the only real hill in town to look at the city lights and holler out over the edge of a cliff where we'd certainly die should we slip. Both locations served as dark parking lots for couples dabbling in love, and that gave one of us an idea (It could have been me). I doubt the son of a high school teacher, or daughter of a dentist, or son of a business owner would have produced a plan so naughty and, in my mind, hilarious.

Let me describe the scene as I remember it - before we wished our teachers and parents would forget. Garvin Heights was no more than a modest hilltop flattened out and paved to offer visitors a grand view of the valley with the rushing Mississippi winding through town and, eventually, to the Gulf of Mexico. On the far side of the view, Wisconsin's rolling bluffs framed the Mississippi Delta. It was lovely in the light of day when we could imagine floating down that mighty river to adventures in cities with more than a half dozen stoplights and a downtown shopping district over four blocks long.

At night, Garvin Heights offered other attractions, namely dark sanctuaries and distance from home. One tall streetlamp cast a circular glow on the pavement. The rest of the hilltop was inky black, with only moonlight to hint at groves of tall oak trees. But once your eyes adjusted, it was easy to see a few cars parked a polite distance from one another. Our gang of five would park as far away from the streetlamp as possible. We'd watch and wait – wait for the couples in the cars to feel safe and anonymous and wait for their car windows to steam up. That was the signal for the curtain to rise.

All car lights off, we silently opened all four doors. On cat feet, we spread out, with each of my friends carrying a roll of bright white toilet paper. In my hand was a German-made viola – a copy of Antonio Stradivarius himself - and a horse-hair bow.

With the enamored couple aware of nothing but their mutual attraction, my playmates quietly and artfully began wrapping the couple's car with toilet paper. I remember being very impressed with Don Burleigh's style. Tall, thin, and lithe, he danced around the target vehicle and delicately placed long trails of TP, dropping them like flower petals. That was the signal for my performance.

I lifted my viola to my chin and began to play. The deep resonance of the low G-string and crisp high pitch of the A-string broadcast the right song for the perfect moment:

"Oh, how we danced on the night we were wed,

We vowed our true love, though a word wasn't said.

The world was in bloom, there were stars in the skies Except for the few that were there in your eyes."

Of course, we soon got a reaction from the startled and confused young couple. A signal for our ensemble to dash stage-left to our car into the shadows. We laughed all the way down the dark and winding road. Until the night we were caught. One of our targets followed us down, stopped at a gas station pay phone, and called the police. They arrived with sirens blaring and took us back to the station downtown. We sat together in a cold room with a bright, bare bulb hanging from the ceiling, waiting for our parents and possibly the gas chamber. After apologies (and useless pleading), we were hauled home by angry and confused parents to face the music (as if the concert hadn't been enough).

Punishments were swift – detention for me (not my first) and for the first offenders as well. But Don, the dear and sensitive parking lot dancer, was dealt the cruelest of blows. The high school vice principal revoked his privilege to deliver the commencement speech at our upcoming graduation. Don cried. We hugged him. Apologized. He cried some more. He went back and begged to the principal himself. A straight 'A' student should get a break! He'd never *ever* do anything like that again. He was *so sorry*. He cried in front of the principal, who, to his credit, took mercy and restored Don's speaking privilege.

And Don kept his promise of a turnaround. I learned later that he'd devoted his life to others – signing up for the Peace Corps and spending many years in Africa and elsewhere helping others. I'd like to think his one brush with the law nudged him in that virtuous direction.

And the rest of us? We all reformed, though I still pick up a fiddle, play a few bars of *The Anniversary Waltz,* and occasionally enjoy being a prankster. Some people never learn.

Blizzard in My Mailbox

Christmas Holidays are upon us - intense weeks of cooking, shopping, planning, wrapping, and strategizing about how to keep Uncle Frank away from the liquor cabinet are upon us. There's no need to consult a calendar because evidence started clogging up my mailbox about two weeks ago. Catalogs I never asked for and absolutely don't want (and spend precious minutes of my life trying to figure out if they're recyclable) have arrived as if hatched inside my modest mailbox.

Some of the unwanted material is addressed to Mr. Darby Patterson and features boxer shorts and nose hair tweezers. Ms. Darby puts those in a separate pile. Others from charities and churches tug at my overly empathetic heartstrings with cover images of doe-eyed children looking both lost and found at the same time. I set those aside due to guilt.

Unloading well over a dozen catalogs in a pre-holiday delivery week is typical although I've never given most of the merchants reason to solicit my business. Never ordered a plush animal, flannel robe, thousand-piece puzzle, cheese log, whoopie cushion, or tee shirt emblazoned with "Fish tremble when they hear my name" from any of them. I've stacked up four-foot-high piles of unwanted, full-color slick mags and felt resentful about being a victim/participant in an annual ritual of waste enjoyed only in places of privilege and wealth. And today, I am thinking back to a different era.

Some of you may be old enough to remember days when receiving a catalog in the mail was thrilling. For those of you who are not yet elder grandparents, let me explain. Once upon a time, there was the 1950s. There were limited ways the broader world entered our homes - large console tube radios, telephones with party lines, and black and white television. One notable exciting option was the arrival of a hefty catalog from the Sears and Roebuck Company. The business was started in 1893 in Chicago. Over the decades, the publication sold everything from tools and clothes to entire houses (hauled across country on railroad lines and assembled on your home site). The company launched brands that survive today- Craftsman Tools, Allstate Insurance, and Kenmore, among others.

For those of us tucked into small-town America, receiving a Sears and Roebuck Catalog was akin to a shopping mall (yet to be invented) sitting on the maple coffee table right there in the living room. Family members queued up to turn the pages of the "America's Wish Book" and linger on illustrations and photographs. (The women's underwear section was a favorite with teenage boys). It was a bi-annual book of dreams and cherished as families planned for back-to-school supplies, birthdays, and holidays. Nothing compared to shuffling through the pages and making noise about what you'd like Santa to bring for Christmas. Or the clothes that would make you more popular at school. It was the way the broader world entered our parochial lives. Anticipating the arrival of packages in months to come was even more exciting than listening-in on conversations of neighbors on the party line. For those of you who have only experienced cell phones – I'll spare you the now-useless details of how to listen in without being detected by the neighbor who would tell your mother who would ground you for a week.

Okay – even though the Sears Catalog was huge, its inventory didn't begin to match that available today in the annual blizzard of magazines inviting us to turn the pages and buy, buy, buy. But for some of us, the shopping experience isn't about quantity and selection. And though some of the catalogs I get are appealing in design, they don't spark excitement or inspire my dreams. Collectively, for me, anyway, they become a guilty burden. I feel responsible for thousands of pages of 60 Lb. gloss-text paper that goes directly from the mailbox to the recycle bin.

And rest assured I've investigated how to escape the annual flood of holiday catalogs. Unsurprisingly, it's complicated and challenging to get off mailing lists that you never signed up to receive in the first place. There's a nonprofit, DMA Choice, that will help consumers remove themselves from mailing lists – but the catch is, with so much online shopping, there is no lasting way to stay off those lists. Merchants pay companies to provide them with lists garnered from our online activities, and, well, our email addresses are there for the taking – over and over again.

So, please let me know if you're interested in a specific catalog that's not being addressed to your home. I'll be happy to share mine – Anything Electronic. Hunting whatever. Truffle oatmeal. Designer diapers. Nose rings. Tee Shirts emblazoned with lame humor. Here are a few of my favorites:

"No. you're right. Let's do it the dumbest way possible."

"Chickens, the pet that poops breakfast."

"They say I have two major flaws. 1: I don't listen and; 2. Something else."

"Silence is golden. Duct Tape is silver."

And thanks to the above holiday humor, at least there's a laugh or two in my overstuffed mailbox.

The Morning Watch

Making it slowly up a hill in my neighborhood, my dog Murphy urging me along, we turn a corner and look into the distance. Up near the top, shrouded in morning fog, are a handful of cars parked on a verge of pine needles and dirt. Near the center of the street is a specter, a figure of a woman standing still as the trunks of the pines that hug the road. Many yards down the hill from the woman, I see a young girl, maybe twelve or so, walking toward me, carrying books in her arms and staring studiously down at the pavement.

As I work my way closer, I see the woman is wearing white, perhaps a classic white robe tied at the waist. Her arms are folded across her chest in a gesture that might ward off the chill. Hugging herself as she might hug the girl walking to the school bus stop. She stands still as a statue, watching and waiting.

I think back to when I was the girl's age. By then, I'd been walking to and from school alone for many years. Navigating the town blocks without fear of anything worse than mischievous neighborhood boys being boys. But this is a different day, it seems, even in this rural place I get to live.

I am sure the girl knows that her mother is a foggy Guardian on the street above her. That looking back might encourage her continued protection. That she hopes none of the other bus kidswitness this act of deep love, perhaps mistaking the vigilance as a lack of trust in her.

The fog has lifted some, and we pass the girl. Her head is lowered, looking at her own footfall. I wave and give her a smile. She glances up briefly and politely responds with a tiny wave back.

I hear the school bus in the distance, and the girl's pace quickens. I know when the bus has glided to its stop because the mother turns toward her driveway, her long brown hair dancing just a bit in the breeze. I am close enough now to see her turn her head to glance one more time down the hill, making sure the bright orange bus has her daughter safely onboard.

Mom sees us marching up the hill and gently smiles at Murphy and me. I am struck by the strong resemblance between her and the girl. There is very little difference, save for the years that separate them.

Still hugging herself in the warmth of the robe, she walks down the driveway to her home, protected by a circle of tall cedars. The fog has lifted, and her own day has begun.

Stress - Turning Yin into Yang

My entry into the graduate class of Life happened over the past summer. I turned 77, and two weeks later, this happened:

We reluctantly decided we needed to move from our much loved home at 4000 feet tucked under Cedar trees and nature's many gifts to be closer to the State Capitol, where my husband works as an advocate for mental health. I said goodbye to the deer that visited my bird feeders and trimmed my grass. And to friendly squirrels that came to our yard for daily treats – a few bold enough to sit and beg for peanuts. And to the empty and quiet winding roads where I took Murphy on his daily walks.

Our house sold fast, and due to a bad real estate market, we bought a place that was a big compromise in quality and brimming with hidden challenges we continue to discover. The brighter side? It's in a sweet Gold Rush town closer to the state capitol, but, thankfully, not in the capitol city.

I exhausted all my emotional and physical reserves with the process of moving. The result was an overload of work and worry that I didn't recognize because I've always risen to challenges. But this effort was overtaken by a thing called stress – an emotion that sometimes inspires and other times overwhelms. I got the 'overwhelm' for months after the move. I was crabby, tired, and bummed until I understood my natural response to unwelcome change and extreme demands on both mind and body.

Research on the impacts of stress helped me slowly climb out of the swamp. It also helped that, like lots of people raised Catholic, I was aware of far greater suffering all over the world – and that burden diminished my self-pity. That, along with the metaphorical "Starving children in China" my grandmother reminded me of as a child, I have a good grasp of how fortunate I am.

In retrospect, I learned a lot about mind and body – and changes over time. I'm hoping that sharing a few of those stress-induced discoveries might be useful should you find yourself facing similar challenges.

An essential culprit in debilitating stress is cortisol. On a good day, this stress hormone helps control our moods – from motivation to fear. It's sometimes called "nature's alarm system." On bad days, cortisol release can bring on high anxiety, depression, memory loss, digestive problems, and brain fog. I can attest to experiencing each of these in addition to the opposite of one symptom – weight gain. I lost 15 pounds within three weeks without dieting. So, a good thing to know is that if we listen closely to what the body tells us, the brain might get a clue about what we need to do. Stop, slow down, breathe, take a break, get some help.

The negative physical and psychological impacts of extreme stress can affect us at any age but might be more debilitating to older folks who are experiencing other losses and health concerns. (This was not, I'm pleased to report, relevant in my case). However, through the entire moving, packing, losing, and hauling experience, I did fail to take care of myself. Here are a few guidelines I ignored:

Under extreme stress, we're advised to eat better and wiser. *Me – who cooks when you can't remember which box contains silverware?*

Take deep, slow breaths. *On a good day, this approach is too boring and time-consuming for me to adopt.*

Reduce caffeine intake. *What? Haul boxes without a quick and legal fix?*

Exercise – *Just what do you call climbing stairs with an armload of boxes?*

In short (and seriously), there are plenty of ways to counteract stress – all we need is awareness of what's happening (I had none of that) and prioritizing mental and physical well-being.

Interestingly, researchers say that being older may actually be an advantage in dealing with stress. They say that some of us have already experienced loss, challenges, and change. We've developed resiliency and may be able to bounce back faster than the younger set.

Stress isn't like having a headache or breaking a bone because we experience stress in normal everyday life. It's like a background noise that we handle without conscious effort. Stress can also lead to inspiration, problem-solving, and creativity. Moderate stress may stimulate the brain to solve problems. It can spark the growth of stem cells that improve memory and enhance survival. Think how vital stress was to the development of early humans – constant awareness that a saber-toothed tiger might be lurking in the weeds – sizing you and yours for dinner.

But stress that overwhelms can have the opposite effect. Causing forgetfulness and anxiety and suppressing our survival instincts. Researchers also say extreme stress hormone levels appear heritable. For example, children of Holocaust survivors were born with high cortisol levels.

My personal takeaway is that awareness and attention to mind and body under high stress *is* a survival skill. Knowing that something is not wrong with our bodies and brains but that both need our attention.

Six months after the move, I'm feeling more like my old self. Able to recognize opportunities I didn't have in our previous environment – like diverse people, restaurants, movie theatres, and a Home Depot five minutes away. But more important than that? We've got families of deer that visit our yard daily to dine on grass and leaves. And even better, I'm building rapport with squirrels (watching them as I write this) happily dining on peanuts and looking at me through the window, begging for more.

Here's a thought I've adapted from a quotable person; "Sometimes it's the small and simple things like the scent of the rain, the sound of a loved one's voice or happy squirrels that bring us peace." How might you personalize this simple advice?

Sculpting a firestorm of heroes

I've been engrossed in a special project since the start of the year. Only a few local friends know what I'm up to. I've shared a lot with you – worry, outrage, hope, humor, and comfort. Today, I want to tell you about a dream I'm making come true every time I pick up a handful of clay.

Some of you will remember that we evacuated our home in the mountains as the Caldor Fire consumed 220,000 acres of the Sierra. Upon returning and assessing the damage (relatively minor for us, considering) and once again feeling comfortable, I started to think about the thousands of people – firefighters, law enforcement, neighbors, volunteers from throughout the state – who stepped up to save thousands of homes in communities threatened by the fire.

I'd written several blogs while evacuated. I was on the phone with fire officials and organizations actively working to get us all through a harrowing experience. I knew that countless volunteers and nonprofits kept abandoned animals safe, empty homes secure, evacuated families fed and sheltered. That fire crews fought around the clock to keep the wild, fast-moving fire contained and away from our neighborhoods.

Soon after we all returned, handmade signs appeared along our winding roads, tacked to trees and fences, expressing appreciation for firefighters and other heroes who made it possible for us to have a home to return to - signs that would soon fade in the sun and run in the rain. And knowing that our gratitude would last a lifetime, but those heartfelt messages would soon be gone, I got the idea of creating a public monument in bronze – a tribute to stand for generations.

The concept turned into a plan that consumed my time for over two years. Four panels will be erected on a granite stone base and stand about six feet tall. Each panel depicts an aspect of the Caldor experience – Firefighters, wildlife threatened by the blaze, Native American fire managers and fighters, and air support. It will be the bronze project of my lifetime – more challenging, complicated, and crazy expensive. I was undeterred by these realities. As I write to you, I have all four panels formed in clay – the first in a series of steps toward completion of the "Tribute to the Heroes of Caldor."

Here's the process: I use an oil-based clay that never hardens and apply it onto smooth, thin boards. Using my hands and metal sculpture tools, I create images "in relief" on the surfaces, starting with general forms and working toward details that I hope convey feeling and meaning. I have not counted the hours spent in my studio bent over the boards. I haven't logged the time because sculpting is not work - it's my joy. I feel only gratitude that, late in life, I discovered a modest ability to make something beautiful from no more than an idea.

But this week marks the start of phase two of sculpting for bronze – the demanding process of making a mold of each panel. I'm very lucky to have help from a local friend and master mold maker, Don Demeno, who comes out of his retirement to help me - because the process requires patience (not my strong suit) and decades of experience (even at my age, I'm a novice). First, we'll cover the panel of the firefighters in several coats of urethane – pouring and brushing until the clay is encased in a thick yet flexible slurry. After it hardens, we pull it from the clay. The next step is to melt big pots of casting wax and pour several thin layers into the mold. Once cooled and hardened, the wax is pulled from the mold, and I'll start working with wax tools and heat to make the images as perfect as possible.

Once the wax panels are finished to my satisfaction, I'll hand them over to a bronze foundry where experts with highly specialized skills will take the project from wax to metal. It takes months for the prep process at the foundry to be complete and ready for the final bronze pour. While I wait for that dramatic moment, I'll be doing the least pleasant part of my crazy idea – raising funds through social media and corporate appeals to pay a giant foundry bill. Not surprisingly, I think that begging and creating are not natural bedfellows. But whatever it takes!

PEOPLE

Her Gifts Keep on Giving

Unbidden, I often receive a visit from my grandmother, whom I called "Nana" throughout our lives together. I have her with me despite her death at 70-some years old decades ago. And I've discovered that, as the years passed, how much of her resides within me. Her birthday was (inconveniently) the day after Christmas on a small farm in Wisconsin to a Polish immigrant family of seven children. She never went beyond the sixth grade but, nonetheless, achieved a modest middle-class married life. I have an old black and white photo of her as a young woman, part of a gathering of employees at Hotel Winona near the banks of the Mississippi in Minnesota. She looks a bit coquettish, devilish. Ready to kick up her young heels. That was not the Nana I'd come to know and love.

Not long after that photo was taken, she met an immigrant Englishman who swept her off her feet to become my grandfather. I lived with them, my divorcee mother (a scandal in those days), and little brother in a small two-bedroom house so close to the railroad tracks the house vibrated when freight trains lumbered by. It was an odd family for the era – divorced women were a rarity and, in a Catholic household, a source of shame.

It wasn't until I was a grandmother myself that I recognized that Nana was the de facto head of our family and that she taught me things one never learns in school. Among her guiding beliefs was superstition. I learned that if you drop a fork, you'll be visited by a stranger. I believed this even though our little clapboard house was never open to people outside our core family. No friends or neighbors were welcome beyond the front door despite how many forks I deliberately dropped. She taught me that an itching nose means someone is thinking about you. Knock on wood, black cats crossing your path, walking under a ladder, bad luck comes in threes, breaking a mirror brings seven years bad luck, and stepping on a crack breaks your mother's back. One that stayed with me a lifetime is "Don't laugh too hard. It means you're going to cry." To this day, I have anxiety about too much happiness.

She did her job proudly and dutifully as a housewife. Down in our damp basement with the coal furnace and Speed Queen washer, she fed wet clothes through a wringer before stuffing her apron full of clothespins and hanging the load on the backyard clothesline. Dominating a kitchen smaller than a bathroom in today's homes – she churned out three homecooked family meals a day. I never once heard her complain or ask for help. She was also the keeper of family secrets. Her Polish family's and ours - which was an unconventional one in those days.

The proximity to railroad tracks brought us visitors despite her rule about unwelcome outsiders. Small groups of 'hoboes' who rode the rails etched our address on telephone poles where freight trains briefly stopped on their cross-country journey. She met them on the stoop of our back door and handed them brown bags of food she'd prepared as they waited. But before tending to the down-on-their-luck visitors, she'd hustle my brother and me into a bedroom and shut the door with an order to "Stay right here till I come get you." We looked forward to the visits with a measure of fear, curiosity, and excitement. It was as close to danger as she'd ever let us get. Her dedication to our safety was fierce. Her commitment to the extended family she never bargained for was unflinching. As was her connection to the Polish family of her birth.

We'd occasionally visit her siblings, where Polish was the language of choice. Speaking Polish in Winona was not a badge of honor – it was a family secret. In those days, people didn't linger on a past that included being an immigrant, poor, and members of the underclass. There was a stigma about the Poles who mainly settled on the east side of our little river city and lived in what was then known as basement houses with only a roof and entryway visible.

Outside of family, there was only one passion in her life. She was devoutly Catholic and surrounded us with religious symbols, including an abundant supply of rosaries. The bedroom I shared with my mother and brother displayed a single picture on the wall – An angel hovering above two frightened children as they crossed a swinging bridge over a deep canyon. I believe my Nana thought of herself as the angel's earthly assistant. She demonstrated that when our town faced a tornado. The scream of a blaring siren pierced the walls, and as we headed to the safety of the basement, Nana grasped a vial of holy water and sprinkled all the open windows before descending the stairs.

As an adult, it was easy to dismiss such beliefs as ignorance or pure superstition. I know better today and am grateful for the gifts I received from my Nana. Things big and small. I can make soup from almost anything edible and with no recipe. I became fascinated with languages. I speak passable Spanish and can rattle off phrases in many other languages - that's thanks to hearing Nana and her sisters gossiping and sharing secrets. I have out-of-control empathy – I'm compelled to help when there's a need. I will rescue nearly any animal, including spiders. I view this as an upside (not everyone around me shares this view). I'm almost always cheering for the underdog. I also cannot watch sad, painful, or moving films without a complete breakdown. (Sadly, this deprives my film-loving husband of some serious viewing). I spent a year of my life sculpting Pope Francis, though my Catholicism is well behind me. Also, I can pronounce Polish names such as Pryzlbilsky, Wisniewski, Kowalczyk, and Bysiewicz.

And then there is the dark side of her bequest to me – I still will not open an umbrella in the house. I'm immediately suspicious when I experience a run of good luck or unrestrained joy. I remain wary of happiness.

These things and more are the legacy of Blanche Bronislawa Darby as her 126th birthday approaches. I believe she's in Heaven, keeping everyone safe.

A Haunted Hero

Memorial Day – a time to honor and remember the men and women who served our country in distant wars. Some never returned home. Others came back with visible injuries that changed the course of their lives. And still others came back with invisible wounds that drove and determined their futures.

In wars prior to the 1980s, there was almost no support for troops once they arrived home under the weight of images embedded in memory – ready to be played back in unexpected ways. They held secrets that would never be told. And so many crumbled under the weight of recurrent nightmares from the battlefield.

After seeing medals awarded to my father for his actions in WWII, I wonder if these experiences of courage and grave danger played a role in the arc of my father's life and, by extension, my mother's, my brother's, and mine. What would our lives have been like had he returned as a veteran with memories to be shared? If he'd been able to tell us about how he won his Silver and Bronze stars and the other badges of heroism that now sit in a velvet box tucked into my dresser drawer. Maybe he'd have been set free of the need for alcohol. Not have sought the company of other women. Not have run from a past too painful to face.

Though he fought for freedom in WWII and the Korean War, he came back in the shackles of memories that remained locked for a lifetime.

Here's what I remember: A tall man with dark curly hair climbing the stairs of our apartment in Chamberlain, South Dakota. He'd been a watchmaker at the local Wall Drug Store. There'd been a fire in the building, and he rescued a little suitcase with a white lamb on the front for me. I was about three years old. I can still see him climbing the narrow stairs to the second-floor apartment we'd rented – the suitcase in one hand. I smelled smoke. He smiled at me. That memory, and then one from much later, after he was banished from our lives in Minnesota and came for a brief visit, was all I had. I was maybe six years old. He had a big 1950s sedan, took me for a short ride, and let me sit on his lap and steer. There was a lot of shouting and remonstrations when he returned me to my grandparent's home, where we lived throughout our childhood. It was our last time together for decades. My brother, then a little toddler, never had an opportunity to build a memory of him. The Dad that neither of us really knew was banished.

From then on, it was an occasional phone call to me that was strictly monitored, and a series of birthday presents that kept him alive in my memory and imagination. The silence and mystery surrounding this separation naturally led me to make him a hero, a savior. So much bigger than my life in a tiny, crowded house where railroad tracks across the street were the only hope of something brighter and beyond. Lying in bed, I would dream about jumping on a freight train and setting off to find him.

Twenty years later, I convinced a boyfriend to drive me south to Arkansas and my dad. He was tucked away in a small town at the foot of the Ozarks. And when I saw him walking toward me on a dusty downtown street, those childhood visions of a savior were shattered. In the first hug of decades, I smelled alcohol on his breath. He took me to his home and a woman named Martha. The house was barely furnished. Inside the refrigerator, I found a half-empty fifth of gin and a piece of leftover hamburger. Nothing else. He and Martha left to spend the night at the American Legion Club. I spent the night on a mattress on the floor, and the next morning, before he was awake, I fled.

But that first visit led to more phone calls and, eventually, the news that he'd stopped drinking. I tried again. With my toddler son, we flew east from Sacramento to near Noel, Missouri, and were met by my dad and Martha. He drove a big gray, windowless van. My son and I sat on folding chairs in the back with an overweight dog at our feet. Martha tried to be friendly, but I could tell that we were unwelcome.

We spent a couple of nights at the house he'd moved to after leaving the city where the Legion bar was his second home. On the third night of our visit, he settled into a tattered blue easy chair. An unfiltered cigarette hung from his lips and made the air thick.

He was not the father I'd created. His shoulders were rounded, his hair was sparse and white, but his eyes – they were still the bright blue I'd remembered. He picked up a satin box from the side table and slowly opened it. Inside were medals – a Purple Heart, a couple of distinguished service medals, ribbons, and, wrapped in a velvet cloth, a Silver Star and Bronze Star. He said he'd been on the landing at Normandy. No details. He told me that I "... wouldn't want to know. It's all in the past."

164

With those words, I realized he'd spent his entire life there, in the past, after the wars, still fighting them. The life-altering events that led to the blue box in his hands were daily companions that he'd tried to drive away with drinks and the comfort of women who didn't know or love him. I knew he would take that loneliness and pain with him to his grave. Two years later, I got his last call. He had cancer. Bad. Throat cancer. And, no, he assured me, it wasn't from smoking. His doctor told him that. It was just a month later that he was laid to rest in the Fayetteville National Cemetery. Martha didn't want me there. I didn't go.

So many veterans like my dad are lauded with medals and praise but forever harbor guilt and responsibility for acts we call heroism. I'll never know what my dad did to walk through the rest of his life as a haunted hero. Ribbons and medals don't heal the wounds of memory, loss, and regret.

But awareness of those dangers is finally acknowledged, and the military offers counseling and support to soldiers who went from battlefield nightmares to mental trauma. I'm hopeful that today's veterans and heroes won't carry their burdens for a lifetime, as did the dad I never knew.

A Writer's Block Buster

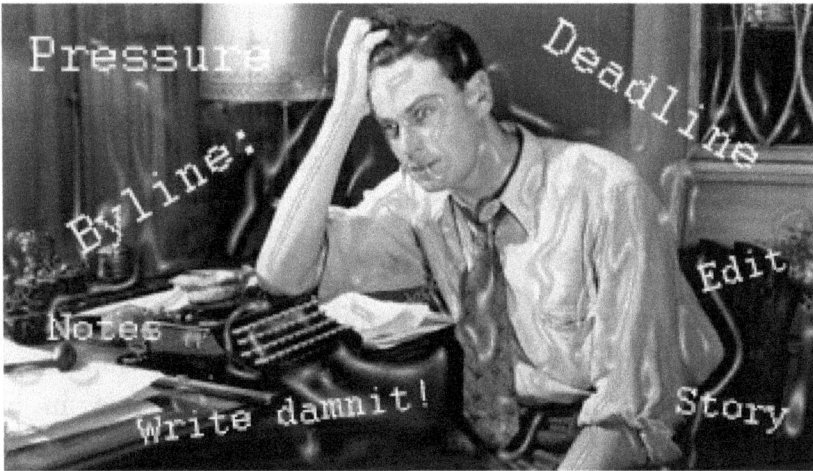

It was not so far past the days when newspaper reporters hunched over their desks with cigarettes dangling from their lips. When the bottom right desk drawer held a fifth of whiskey and a shot glass. On top of the desk, there would be messy piles of paper and stacks of skinny, spiral-bound Reporters' notebooks shoved against ashtrays brimming with crushed butts. The crowning glory was a husky Underwood typewriter eating up ribbons of spooled carbon.

This was the original newsroom known to Ken Harvey, who became the Executive Editor of the *Sacramento Union,* where I landed a job in the late 1980s. Ken came equipped with decades of experience and a sardonic sense of humor that was at odds with the conservative newspaper where Mark Twain had once published his pieces. Of course, a lot had changed by then – offline computers were used to input stories, for example. But others hadn't – the tension of a newsroom, the constant chatter and taunts of reporters, the drive to deadlines and competition for the front page.

It was there that I got my basic and best education as a journalist. And I remember the following experience as a breakthrough lesson delivered by Ken Harvey in just six words.

I'd burst into the newsroom smelling of smoke from the dense forest fire I'd been covering for more than a week. I rushed to my desk and threw down my gear. I was darn sure I'd end up on the coveted above-the-fold front page. The newsroom hummed like a tuned engine, with dozens of reporters busy pounding on the keys, stampeding toward deadline.

I sat down and stared at my blank screen. The little white cursor blinked against a green field waiting to be populated with my story about the wildfire that burned more than 60 homes in the nearby Sierra, the forest service plane carrying retardant that crashed and killed its crew, the 1400 firefighters camped out for more than a week of exhausting, dangerous duty. I'd been there from day one, taking notes, recording voices, choking on smoke, and running from flames.

I looked at my notebook and flipped through the pages, thinking. What's my lead? How do I grab the reader without being sensational? Do I start with the cargo plane? I'd been there only minutes after the crash …. Where to start …. The cursor continued to jump.

"Darby!" The sharp voice of Ken Harvey broke my concentration on how to begin what might be the biggest story of my blossoming career in journalism. I looked up.

"Why aren't you writing?" Ken barked.

"I'm thinking ... getting my notes organized," I answered defensively.

"Well, stop thinking and start writing!"

"It's just a little writer's block; I'll get over it!" I whined.

Ken folded his arms and loomed over my desk. "You've got writer's block, and I've got a deadline. Choose! You can't have both!"

I turned to the screen and started tapping the keys. The story pretty much wrote itself and months down the road, when blades of fresh green grass were pushing up through the ground of the charred Sierra where I'd spent a week covering the fires, I won a journalism award for my series.

The advice from Ken to choose between writer's block and a deadline carried me through the rest of my life as a reporter and writer. I never missed a deadline or cogitated long on how to start. As I migrated to other, better-paying writing posts, I kept his admonition in mind each time I sat and struggled to begin yet another story. Just 'do it' was, and is, my mantra.

I've found that searching my creative conscience is generally a waste of time, an indulgent luxury that reporters can't have because they face deadlines. This same philosophy applies to creative writing. How many people are stuck on their great idea for a book but never get past the planning phase? Plenty, I've discovered.

Ken Harvey taught me (and countless other reporters) that the act of writing is a living process that begins to breathe with words on a surface. That visual reality inspires like pondering never will. Ken died a few years ago, but his influence lives on. I feel him loom over my shoulder every time I find myself staring at a blank screen. And I wish that I'd let him know about the legacy he'd left to me.

Though I no longer work on tight deadlines, I still pound out words as if my 'job' depends on it. And, at the end of each session, I have tangible proof that a deadline can be a lifeline for working writers. Thanks, Ken Harvey, for giving me that and more.

The Fishy Boyfriend
Who Got Away

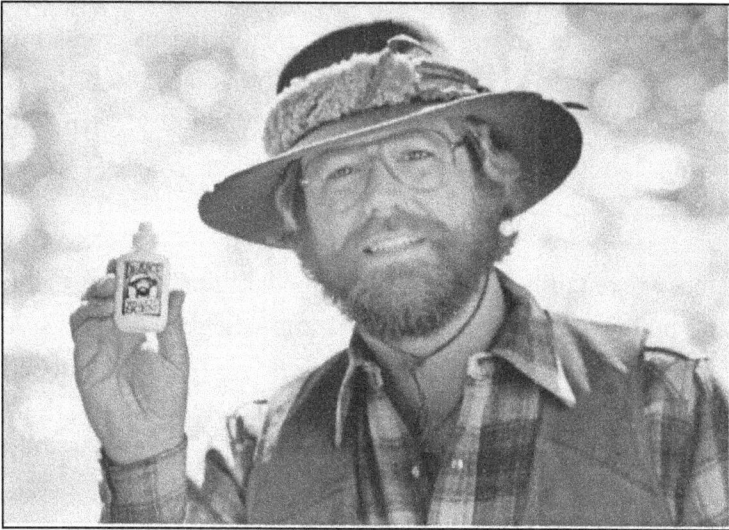

When you're a child, you feel as if you're pretty much living a normal life. Not much is exceptional or memorable. I'm sure that's why I never questioned my friendship with a neighborhood boy named Greg Bambenek. In my childhood memory, Greg was fun, interesting, cute, mischievous, and unexceptional. He was my best friend from about age eight to 13 (when I felt it wasn't acceptable to be hanging out with a boy a whole year younger than me).

It took nearly 50 years for me to realize that Greg was always exceptional. Today (among many other things), Greg is known as the inventor of Dr. Juice – scented bait designed to attract specific fish. His brand is sold worldwide. But Greg is also a practicing psychiatrist, a survival-level outdoorsman, a musician, and an adventurer. We found each other again online – now, as grandparents on opposite sides of the country.

In talking with him, I got to revisit our shared past in a quiet, landlocked Minnesota town when I thought it was normal that Greg should chase me with garter snakes and trap me in the limbs of his backyard tree for hours at a time. Or that I would trust him enough to allow him to blindfold me, walk me down his basement stairs and into position, and then remove the blindfold. My 10-year-old self faced a beaver hanging upside down, disgorging his intestines six inches from my nose. Or that walking into his upstairs room would set off flashing lights, a siren, firecrackers, and gales of laughter from Greg.

Later, when we were young teenagers, Greg and I ran through a warren of tunnels under our local high school to sneak into a lecture by the noted Wernher Von Braun - the former Nazi scientist turned Director of the Marshall Space Center. The man whose post-war vision infused America's space program with innovations and made him a controversial national hero. To this day, I have no idea what Von Braun said that day. He may as well have been speaking Martian (a planet he suggested visiting within his lifetime). I understood precisely none of it. I only knew that the moment was important and, more importantly, adventurous. Greg, however, sat transfixed, cradling his curly blond head in his hands, eyes sparkling, nodding now and then with understanding. I do recall checking my friend out in a new way, thinking he was kind of cute but still a whole year younger than me. Not boyfriend material.

After graduating high school, Greg studied medical science with the goal of becoming a doctor of psychiatry. For most people, this academic quest would be strictly books and papers and endless tests. But, as a pre-med college student, Greg managed to land a research project that led to his spending many months in Vietnam, Thailand, India, and China, where he learned to speak Mandarin, and studied acupuncture and Chinese medicine. In Southeast Asia, he conducted research on marijuana use among American troops fighting the Vietnam War and did related assessments for government agencies and the World Health Organization. This quest for knowledge took him to Kathmandu, Kolkata, New Delhi, Kabul, and beyond.

In those travels, Greg experienced being tossed into a car with a band of drug dealers under attack by rivals, saved the life of a young American woman in Nepal who'd overdosed on Hippie-era drugs and hooked up with a redheaded woman from America who (wearing a brown wig) attempted to steal medical secrets from a researcher in Nepal. In the Indian city of Agra, Greg fought off a gang of young men who sexually harassed his female companion. His next stop was the Taj Mahal, where he played his guitar, setting off an echo that reverberated for an entire minute. All this, and more, before officially entering medical school.

As a practicing psychiatrist, Greg worked as medical director of a Native American treatment center in Minnesota and other human service venues while continuing his world travels. One trip took him to Belize, where he met an indigenous Mayan fisherman who baited his line with scents from local plants and small jungle critters. Fish were easily caught using a line and hook with a piece of scented cloth attached. That launched Greg's next identity as Dr. Juice.

Much of Greg's childhood was spent at his father's side fishing, hunting, and exploring the natural environment. Rivers, lakes, and forests provided not only food for his family but also a deep understanding of the natural world. He put that history and the experience with the Mayan fisherman together, spent months in his lab examining the physiology of various fish – specifically their olfactory systems - and developed his own pheromone-based fish bait. The result was Dr. Juice Fish Scent - irresistible to fish and to anglers all over the world. The *New York Times* and *Wall Street*

Journal even wrote articles about Dr. Juice. At least one U.S. President also chose the bait for a fishing trip after Greg tested George H. Bush's fingers for a scent that would either attract or repel fish when he applied bait to a hook (the Secret Service dudes at Bush's side were not pleased). Results of that test may explain why the former President (an avid fan of angling) didn't have much luck as a fisherman.

Greg lives in a spacious cabin on the edge of the largest lake in the world – Lake Superior in Northern Minnesota, where no fish is safe from Dr. Juice.

We remained in touch, and are working on turning his life into a book. It's a grand circle, from the backyards of a block in the midwest to where we both are today – me in California and Greg living in the far north of Minnesota on the edge of Lake Superior. His health took an unfortunate turn in the past several months, but we are chipping away at a life story that's a mix of adventure, mischievousness, discovery, and dedication.

Time and distance change many things, but I'm grateful that some memories never fade. And one day in the near future, Greg and I will appear together again – from our forever friendship to our book about an exceptional life.

Dancing Her Way Home

Mollie Burrows was a dear friend and role model for me. She died at the age of 97, having relished life and with very few regrets. I recall only two. A complaint about one of many boyfriends she'd had since retiring and another relating to how long she waited to fix her nose. She told me that, for most of her life, she'd felt "ugly." That men didn't often ask her out on a date. Sometime in her 60s, she made a bold move, visited a cosmetic surgeon, and found herself in demand.

"I'm telling you," she said to me, "I was ugly as an old fence. Then I got my nose done. I only wish I'd done it sooner." Well into her 90s, Mollie would laugh and tell me about her late-in-life beaus, joyfully recounting her dates and dancing and singing – and still holding out hope of a new romance.

Molly lived alone in a second-story apartment accessed by a set of concrete stairs that scared everyone but her. I remember celebrating her 92nd birthday with her, in which she indulged in a cocktail and two glasses of wine. It was the only time she agreed to let someone escort her up those stairs.

On her 95th, Mollie rented a ballroom and threw herself a birthday bash, complete with a deejay spinning all her favorites. She was resplendent in a striking blue evening dress with a pearl necklace, her makeup just so. Mollie's always-perfect blonde hair was swept into a bouffant of waves reminiscent of movie queens of the 1950s. To ensure she'd fully enjoy the evening, she hired a lithe, debonair dance instructor wearing a tux to be her partner for the evening. "I don't like to stumble around with men who can't dance," she told me. "It's a waste of my time."

When I first had the fortune to meet her, she was already in her 80s and knew absolutely what her life was about. She'd reminisce about the war years when she lived in Berkeley and danced with GIs on weekends. I'm pretty sure that's where she developed an encyclopedic memory for songs she could sing word-for-word - and often did. This love of tunes from the 30s to the 60s was something we shared, along with a passion for the dignities and rights of aging.

Mollie was a pioneer in the movement to demand respect for the elders among us. Nothing made her angrier than to have someone call her "dear" or "sweetie" or talk down to her as if she didn't hear or understand, strictly based on her age. Thus, Mollie was great company when I had a few speaking engagements with Eskaton to talk about ageism in America. Mollie said over and over again – that *this* is the new frontier of discrimination. Together, we made business cards to hand out to young transgressors that offered them advice: *"I am not your sweetie, not your dear, not your honey. I am not your young lady. Been there, done that! I am your elder. Thank you for your respect."*

Mollie lived a fierce life and didn't slow down her pace even after she agreed to move into an independent living community at the age of 94. For the first few weeks, she was a specter of anger about the move, and her dislike of the place laced every conversation with those of us who had urged her to move to a safer environment. But in her irrepressible fashion, she soon found ways to enjoy the company of her agemates. While she still would curse about the meals served in the dining room, she lauded the residents. "You would not believe what some of these people have done," she told me. "They're amazing. Accomplished. No one should ever sell them short!" She even joined the daily exercise program but dropped out after a week, "I like my own routine," she said. "Theirs is too easy. Not challenging. Wimpy." She raised her own profile by starting a weekly competition of the musical game "Encore." Every lyric to every song before 1965 and beyond. No one could beat her. Mollie was also one of the first people to read my mystery book. I asked what she thought. "Well, I really enjoyed it," she said. "It's just as good as any of those books you pick up at the grocery store!" I was thrilled with that review and included it in my publicity.

Our world is populated with Mollies – people who've lived long, robust lives and carry with them stories, memories, experiences, and wisdom that only time and distance can build. People who can teach us all a great deal. There was a time in our history when family life was structured to let that happen naturally. Before the Industrial Revolution, elders were the source of inherited wealth and trades. They served as head of the family, making decisions and building value throughout their lives and then passing on the baton.

The dynamic is vastly different now, but not the reality. Elders still retain the value that only accrues with time and experience. If only we are smart enough to listen.

Missing the Moment but Alas, Not the Man

It was decades ago, and I was about to acquire yet another new husband. He was fit for Hollywood. Tall, green eyes, tousled blond hair, the body of an Olympian. He had an animal charisma – a one-time Green Beret in Vietnam with a gold tooth that shot off sparks of sunlight when he smiled – which was often. Jake was a medic in some of the hottest war zones of that era and, indeed, arrived in my life with full-on PTSD, though it hadn't yet been officially identified.

Like all the men I'd gathered in my life that didn't work out as intended, Jake regularly shot out cues that something was amiss, and I quickly dismissed them for the very basic, shallow reasons outlined above. An early hint of abnormality happened on our first date – which was no more than a drive in his old blue-green sedan in which we laughed a lot and flirted our way to next steps. We arrived at my house well before dark and sat talking in the car, me thinking, 'should I invite him in, or is it too soon?'

I checked out his profile – strong jaw, perfect nose, and smile quick to flash like fireworks. He was impish, mischievous – just enough trouble to interest me, a reporter attracted to the edgy, potentially dangerous opportunities in life. He routinely wore Army greens that matched his eyes. Who was I to resist temptation?

Just as that wholly unjustified thought skidded through my brain, Jake said, "Can you give me a minute, baby," (Baby? Wow, Swoon). "I need to rest my eyes." Like slow-motion animation, he lowered his curly head to my lap and fell soundly asleep. I sat dazed for a minute, wondering what to do and how to feel. Then the love brain kicked in, and I decided he was exhausted after his day nursing vets at a hospital 90 minutes away. Nothing unusual about that. I wrapped an arm around his shoulder and sat there, trapped by his upper body and my most basic instincts. I felt the constant rhythm of his breathing and watched tiny movements in his left eye as dreams paid him a visit. The moment grew to a half-hour, and he showed no sign of waking. Boredom overtook my fascination. I coughed a few times and nudged him awake.

Throughout the months of our whirlwind relationship, this narcoleptic behavior continued. He could fall asleep nearly anywhere, anytime. Routinely, we'd be driving somewhere, and he'd pull to the side of the road for a 15-minute nap. I spent that downtime remembering waking and romantic moments like this one:

178

We were on the peak of the roof of an old barn on his piece of property in the country. The sky was swirling with clouds that promised to hold off rain until we'd finished shingling. Wind blew hard at our hair and clothes, but we joyfully worked. Me on the north side of the peak, and Jake at the opposite end. He looked at me and shouted through the weather – "Baby, this is life!" and the gold tooth sparked like a flash of lightning. I felt like a pioneer woman, staking out the homestead on untamed acres in the company of a battlefield hero building back his life after the horrors of war, with me straddling the roof and wielding a hammer as if I'd be born with it gripped in my little pink fist. This land (would be) *our* land.

Just for a moment, my eyes fell to the ground. There, a gutted deteriorating farmhouse awaited my touch, as well as a roof and plumbing. A garden was dreaming of sprouting from the earth suffocated by weeds and sheltering snakes. At least a quarter of Jake's five acres was littered with cars in various stages of decay – sports cars without doors or hoods, a couple of station wagons sans wheels or windows. The interiors sheltered a variety of chickens, and a noisy red rooster occupied the back half of an old, rusted-out fire truck. Other vehicles (collectibles, Jake told me) laid flat on the dirt with doors dangling hopefully from frames. An old military-style Jeep sat tilted on a mound of car parts and held two buckskin goats sitting on the wire coils of seats that had once held soldiers. Jake said they were investments in his future (the cars, not the goats and chickens).

The reality of the evidence surrounding me almost permeated the warm glow of the moment. But then the wind kicked up, and a light rain started to fall. Jake stood tall on the roof, hammer in one hand; he opened his arms wide in an encompassing embrace of it all. His farm so full of potential, the churning sky, the woman with starry eyes hugging the roof between her knees.

With the wind beating against his body, he walked the peak to me, his khaki shirt flying open, a smile broad as the valley below.

He stretched an arm down to me and pulled me up in an embrace. There we stood, frozen and warm. MGM could have been filming with an orchestra dancing on the wind.

Of course, reality was bound to kick in, even in a delusional, love-struck brain like mine. I came to realize the truth of my mythological man – along with the funny and adventurous, there was damage done by what life had handed him. A trigger temper, hints of abuse in former relationships, battlefield trauma from America's shameful war.

But it was an affair of the heart to remember, and I artfully dodged Cupid's sharpest arrow. Among the benefits of this brief affair was a character I included in my mystery novel, *The Song of Jackass Creek* – in it, Jake works at the local dump, drives the mountain town's ambulance, and occasionally saves lives. Not so far from the truth to make it a lie.

Pigeons, Portraits, and a Mystery

To this day, so many years later, I don't know how to think about the experience I'm sharing with you. There was no high drama or humor, no lesson to be taken away, yet the visit to the old, whitewashed home at the end of a long dirt road up the hill from Redbud remains a vivid memory.

I'd seen Willie in Redbud many times, driving into town on his golf cart on the same road traveled by 60-ton log trucks. They shared the narrow winding road from Redbud up to Strawberry Mine, where it abruptly ended at an elevation of 7,500 feet. No one ever spoke of a near miss or complained that the unstable little cart was not road-worthy. No traffic tickets were issued, and sheriff's deputies simply gave Willie the standard Redbud high sign when they met on the road (an index finger almost imperceptibly raised from the steering wheel).

Willie drove the golf cart because he was not physically able to drive a regular car. He walked with crutches, his body bent oddly at the waist, and people explained his condition as "some kinda Polio." He walked mainly through using upper body strength to pull the rest of himself forward, leveraging the crutches. The hand controls on his golf cart gave him mobility so that he could make the occasional visit to town.

Word in the Eagle's Eye Cafe was that Willie raised pigeons, prize pigeons. I thought his story would make a good human-interest piece in my weekly paper, *The Timberline Times,* and got myself an invitation to visit.

To say that the road into his place was unimproved is an understatement. As the crow flies, it was maybe two miles off the main road, but the twists and turns took it to more like five, ending at a homestead with outbuildings in various stages of surrender. Willie's golf cart was parked near the front door of the family house. No other vehicles were in sight. I thought how lonely Willie must be - disabled and alone with only pigeons for company.

I stuck my head inside the door and called his name. "In here," I heard and lugged my recorder and SLR camera toward the voice. I wandered to an arched doorway that opened to a living room. There, I saw an elder man in a hospital bed shoved next to a window with only a fringe of white hair escaping from the sheet that wrapped around him. A second man, who looked both old and young at the same time, sat in a chair on the opposite side of the room, staring at the ceiling. In the middle of the room was Willie, leaning on his crutches. I saw no television or radio, and, except for the continual cooing of pigeons and the remarkably fine oil portraits that adorned the walls, the atmosphere was not unlike that of a mortuary.

Willie wasn't much of a talker, and it was obvious he wasn't used to company. He didn't offer introductions or an explanation for the body in the bed (though I assumed it was alive), and I tried to compensate by asking questions. How long had he lived there (forever), did he ever feel lonely (nope), and asked about the artwork. "Who did these pictures? They're wonderful!"

Willie pulled himself over to one wall. "You recognize anyone?" He asked. I did, indeed. Marylin Monroe, Elvis, Rock, Betty. A whole gallery of expertly done portraits of stars from the

40s and 50s. Willie said the paintings were done by his dad, who, in his youth, was a successful artist in Hollywood. People had paid him well for their portraits, and many ended up in the homes of Hollywood glitterati. I was also hoping for an explanation that would tell me how he and the silent company in the living room landed in a vast, dilapidated house hidden in the pines with the simple question. As a star reporter, I asked, "So, how did you end up here?"

I'm always here," he said. "You want to see my friends now?"

I glanced around the room once more. The mute man in the chair hadn't acknowledged me. The body under the sheet had not stirred.

I followed Willie outside to a big oak tree outfitted with two-by-fours nailed into the trunk as a ladder that ended at a platform about 18 feet up. Willie dropped his crutches to the ground and grabbed hold of a sturdy rope that hung from the platform. He pulled himself up the ladder, arm over arm, one rung at a time. I followed and joined him on the platform where boxes and cages were assembled into an avian apartment complex. The residents were not startled at his appearance, nor mine. They sat cooing and preening and cocking their little heads in calm curiosity.

Willie again displayed a loquaciousness that seemed totally out of character. He explained the differences and similarities among the birds. He made clicking sounds to include them in the conversation. He plucked a few from their perches and petted their silky feathers with tenderness. "They come back," he said. "They always come right back here." No, they were not homing pigeons, he added. Just pigeons who knew where home was.

I got lots of great photos that day - black and whites that seemed to fit both the birds and the cinematic atmosphere in which

I'd landed. A few decades later, I still remember the otherworldliness of my visit. No doubt the old man shrouded in the sheet is long gone – and likely Willie, the paintings, and the creaking old house. I wonder, did generations of pigeons linger on, making use of the safehouse tucked into the limbs of the big oak tree? Do they teach generations of chicks about the twisted, kind little man who came with food, cooing and clucking at them like one of their own? I want to believe that.

Policy Wonk at Work,
Artist in the Kitchen

I've been waiting and watching to take in this country's reaction to our extreme ownership and near-religious worship of firearms. When I write to you about the issue, I want to focus on something deeper than the numbers and our historically embedded attitudes. I don't want to repeat the same old tropes we've all heard before. So in place of prematurely publishing my thoughts, I'm offering you a contrast to politics and controversy – a spousal tale wrapped up in a recipe.

My husband and I are opposites in many ways – and this may be the same for you and your partner in life. I am spontaneous, generally disorganized, extremely visual, and hopelessly creative. It's these flaws and/or blessings that keep me in love with writing and completely engaged with my passion for sculpting. My husband, Randall, is scheduled and organized, has attention to and retention for detail, and is comfy surrounded by what I would see as distracting chaos (notes on the floor, open books, piles of paper, etc.). He's a mental health policy expert and widely regarded as an advocate and authority. He can recall legislation, landmark events, names, dates, bill numbers (i.e., AB123), and other detailed information with Wikipedia accuracy. Me? Please don't ask me for the Google phone number I've had for years because I can't remember it.

We take these disparities into other parts of our lives. I'm the weekday cook – and, honestly, to call what I do 'cooking' might be stretching the meaning of the word. If I accidentally throw together something delish, it is not reproducible because the recipe is spontaneous – like finger-painting when you're a kid. Conversely, Randall cooks like a professional with a culinary vision that leads to extraordinary results on the dinner table. He designs flavors, uses ingredients I've never heard of, and develops a step-by-step plan for success. He also makes one hell of a mess in the kitchen. If red sauce is involved, the whole room resembles a murder scene when he's done. And then there's his love of high-fire cooking, which gives ingredients a smokey richness. The method also sets off smoke alarms and occasionally results in an actual fire, which, thus far, has been confined to the stovetop or to the dish towel he uses to manipulate the pots on the stove.

Sometimes, I sit at the island in our kitchen and work on some clay as he's cooking. It's fun to watch someone lost in their art – Randall buzzing around the room in his chef's apron, a towel draped over his shoulder, cookbook open, and ingredients strewn across the countertops. He's keenly focused on his creation, as I am on mine. He makes trips to our herb garden and brings in handfuls of carefully selected varieties to complement the dish. The kitchen takes on the fresh smell of thyme, oregano, rosemary on the vine. He carefully pulls leaves from fragile stems and crushes or dices according to his culinary vision. I take credit for planting the herb garden and making it look artistic. I cannot tell the difference between rosemary and thyme or basil and oregano. I once chopped up a weed and put it in a dish (okay, maybe more than once, but who's counting).

Sitting there, listening to Spanish guitar streaming to the kitchen speaker, I feel as if I'm in a foreign film, one that will move from the stove to the table and out to a cobbled street where Randall and I will Tango as a Mediterranean sun sinks into the sea. But that's where my romantic brain goes and why I'm far too distractible to cook like he does. But it would be a beautiful ending to the story, right?

When the cooking, baking, searing, turning, and timing are done, the results on the dinner table are award-winning. I sit with my back to the stove, looking out at a patio, and beg Randall to remember the recipe and write it down. And I know that behind me, there is another achievement. The stove and countertops, and sink area are a disaster zone, as if a tiny tornado blew through, tipping pots and pans and splattering sauces from wall to counters to floor and out the window, which is open because of the potential for the kitchen fire.

But please understand that I am not complaining. I am only reporting the results and facts as I see them. Most important throughout the spousal cooking event is that Randall, who fights for far more than 40 hours a week to improve and protect mental health care, gets to escape into his creative mind and make a deliciously good mess.

Memories Molded from Hollywood to the Hills

We're in Don DeMenno's garage across the road from a bounteous Apple orchard – one of many that bring tourists to the Gold Country hills year-round. But we are worlds and centuries away while in Don's garage/studio. Don is a master mold maker who's worked for some of this country's most accomplished bronze sculptors. His skill took many years to master and a temperament that I lack – one that's largely centered on patience.

I've brought Don a panel for the Caldor Tribute monument I'm making to honor the countless people who saved our mountain homes from the ravages of last year's forest fire that consumed 225,000 acres. The work starts with clay images sculpted on a piece of 4-ft. by 2-ft. plywood. I'm making six panels (three two-sided bronze depictions of aspects of fighting the fire. When I'm done with a panel, we next make a urethane mold – a negative of my positive clay images. It's a messy, sticky, hands-on process that takes about a half-day of work for each panel.

We combine two gallon-sized containers of viscous liquid components that interact and start a process of slowly hardening to a flexible, rubbery consistency that is a perfect mold of the clay relief I've done on the panel. We've framed the panels so that we can pour a few layers and later use brushes to capture the texture of details. Once dry, we pull the mold off the clay (all my sculpting work is history and discarded), and the negative image is ready for the next step – applying melted casting wax to once again make a positive image.

Throughout the process, I try to watch and listen so that my own skills improve (a lot of room for that) and also because Don is fascinating. A man who practices a very ancient craft that reaches back into 6000 years of human history and whose personal memories of Hollywood in the 1950s and '60s are as vivid as the golden screen. Let me start with a short description – To the casual observer, Don is a quiet man, not one to draw attention to himself. He's methodical, patient, never asks for attention or praise. Not seeking the spotlight. But through our many hours of mold making, I've been amazed and entertained by this meek man who puts up with my impatience and teaches lessons in art and life.

Don was born in New York, the son of Italian immigrants. His uncle, 'Jock' Giranda, had a gig with Cecil B DeMille in New York and followed him to Hollywood when the famous producer moved his operation. Don's family also relocated to glitzy Los Angeles. By that time, his uncle had already been a stunt rider and a jockey. He was a great introduction to the magic of Hollywood.

Don's teenage years were filled with sightings of movie stars and opportunities to take part in the scene. He remembers filling in the crowd for a Dick Clark TV (American Bandstand-fame) summer show that filmed daily. He recalls that Paul Revere and the Raiders was the house band, lip-syncing their music.

"They wanted a crowd, a background of a bunch of kids whooping and hollering," Don explained. On one trip to Universal Studios, the teenage Don found himself having lunch in the commissary with actor Jimmy Boyd – the kid who made the song "I Saw Mommy Kissing Santa Claus" a nationwide hit. He also appeared in "Inherit the Wind" in 1960. The film used the 1925

"Monkey" Trial that focused on creationism to highlight McCarthyism. The young Boyd testified:

*"**Howard:** He said that men sort of evaluated from Old World monkeys.*

__Matthew Harrison Brady:__ Do you hear that, friends? Old World monkeys! According to Bertram Cates, we don't even descend from good American monkeys!"

Before Don's lunch was over, the star gazing got even better – Doug McClure (the rugged cowboy in the 1960s hit series *The Virginian*) came and sat down with them. And then the entire crew of *McHale's Navy* walked by, led by Academy Award-winning actor Ernest Borgnine. But the day offered even more.

After lunch, Don's party of four walked into a dark rehearsal studio with just one person framed by a bright spotlight – Doris Day was rehearsing a dance. Don met her and shook the star's hand. On other occasions, he encountered Ray Charles, and Ike and Tina Turner.

Don went to the nightclub (once named the Moulin Rouge), where he opened the lobby door for Robert Vaugn – the "*Man From Uncle.*" And then there was the chat he had with Charlton Heston at a studio party and the chance encounter with James Darin – they "talked motorcycles," Don remembers. One of Don's favorite pastimes was cruising Hollywood and Sunset Boulevards on his Honda 150.

My friend talks about these brushes with fame while smoothing out urethane and touching up things I've done that don't meet his professional standards. It's not bragging when he talks about his Hollywood days – it's joyful mental meandering to relive moments far different than those we might expect today – in a mountain village, isolated from city life. Where there are more trees than people and one lonely movie theater miles away.

But now it's Don DeMenno who has the audience. I'm amused and fascinated by his tales of youth and Hollywood and 24-hour days in which the stars shone brightly. At the same time, we're making art together – me learning and Don teaching. When the afternoon is over, Don wipes his hands with a half-sheet of paper towel and carefully cleans his tools, returning them to their particular places. I've got urethane stuck to my arms above my elbows, blobs of rubber drying on my jeans and shoes. It's also in my hair.

I'm grateful for his patience with impatient me. And for sharing stories about encounters with movie stars whose names and faces were only distant technicolor dreams to a small-town girl from Minnesota. When the near-impossible dream of the Caldor Tribute stands tall on our mountain, we'll have a new memory that's shared.

The Best Uncle I Never Had

Uncle Bob came into my life driving a half-ton bearing signs of countless trips to the local dump. You'd think a guy might not be able to load enough discarded stuff into the bed to make the job financially viable. But Uncle Bob – the moniker he gives himself in ads in our local, small-town shopper – has many talents. Among them is spatial acuity and the ability to balance anything atop a table leg. He shows up in a signature flannel shirt, working man's khakis, and a cap stained with time and toil.

My husband and I circle around to help him load – there's some heavy, awkward junk in our pile. Uncle Bob slows us down with a calming voice. "Now, I don't want you to rush," he says. "Take your time. I'm never in a hurry. We've got plenty of room."

Uncle Bob is old enough to be a great-grandparent. Yet, one of his biggest concerns is the "seniors" in his community. "You know," he says to me, "Some of those seniors just don't even have the means to provide for themselves." So – as a determined agemate – he takes items that might be useful to folks not as active as he is to strategic spots where someone in need might make good use of them: senior communities, trailer parks, and such.

Uncle Bob assesses my messy pile of items that range from crushed boxes to unloved furniture and board games we meant to play and never did. He slips on work gloves and starts loading, seemingly without a plan. When my husband questions the ability of his rig to carry the enormous load we have, Uncle Bob smiles and reassures us it will be a "piece of cake."

I know that behind his humble appearance, there's a lifetime of personal and financial success. He's an old-school entrepreneur with online savvy and a way with people. In earlier years, he worked with California's transportation agency and later branched out to entrepreneurial ventures.

"I sell six or seven programs and mail out 200 or 300 letters a month to people all over the U.S. and Canada," he explains. "It helps people make extra money. " Leapfrogging from that early success, he launched into a life-changing venture. "Then I got into real estate, and I bought properties here and there, and I'd flip them, you know. That was back when you could buy 50 or 60 acres for forty-thousand dollars." He arranges a broken chair atop the growing pile and stuffs a decorative pillow between the legs. "I have the gift of gab – which you can probably tell." He laughs at his confession. "That was back in the 80s. You can't do that now," he adds. He reports all this while simultaneously loading large and small items, nestling them together like a 3D puzzle master. He makes a place for everything – from tables and chairs to kids' toys, building materials, lampshades, and no longer-loved clothes.

He philosophizes while topping the spontaneous sculpture. "Anyway, I think people should work until they're 150," (insert one of many chuckles). "So long as they enjoy what they're doing! That's what I told my daughters. I said, find out what you enjoy doing and then add value to it. And you'll never have to work another day in your life!"

My husband is glancing up at the marvelous mound that's reaching well over cab height. Uncle Bob reassures him. "No worry. It's all good." Another chuckle spills out as he starts to tie down the load. He's using a thin rope – one that I might use to tie a return package to Amazon.

Circling the truck and looking for crevices to fill with pieces of old lumber, Uncle Bob tells me he's looking forward to the afternoon. He's got it perfectly planned to include what he calls a "treat."

"It's my football day," he says through a smile. "I love juicing! I got apples, carrots, parsley, cucumber. I make a big bunch and put ice in it, and it lasts me through the whole football game. That's my treat." His face beams with excitement.

He continues - "Once you start juicing, you feel so good!" He contrasts his treat with the common American snack – meat and cheese. "You're getting everything you need, and it's all concentrated. I'm having a great affair with my juicing machine." He laughs and launches into beatitudes of juicing as a hobby. "I study it on my computer. I mix vegetables with fruit – 1 sometimes the vegetables don't taste so good – like spinach." He makes a sour face. "You just add apple to it, and you don't even taste the spinach. I do a lot of research."

He tucks the end of the rope deep into the pile and circles around his pickup. Satisfied, Uncle Bob slips off his work gloves and says, "Well, Darby, I think we got it. I'm glad you remembered me."

As if I could forget? I say, "You're unforgettable."

He chuckles. "I've had people tell me that!"

\#

Burning Man Fest Comes to the Kitchen

For some reason I feel an urge to talk about observations I've gathered through countless dinners with male cooks, some of whom have been husbands (don't ask, I won't tell).

Let me also add that I've conducted a survey via social media and gathered input from the partners of men whose cooking often results in rave reviews. This is not a column about the quality of cuisine but more about those dishes, pots, pans, and surfaces involved in the creative cooking process.

But I feel like I'm dithering now, avoiding the launch into a topic that women share (with affection) with each other but know enough not to reveal to the male who launches a coup in the kitchen. And as a final caveat, let me add that the following comments are only specific to my personal observations and those of women whose stories I solicited and that no husbands will be harmed or identified (with the exception of mine) in the process.

Let me begin with a personal experience named John - a handsome, uber-male, former Green Beret who turned my tiny kitchen into a war zone littered with innocent victims. The guy liked to call me "Baby" – a clue to his attitude about women that I should have immediately grasped. It was, of course, a meal centered on beef, a slab as big as Rhode Island. He jabbed the bloody hunk with a barbeque fork and waved it at me. "Look at this, Baby, this is what you call a cut of meat!" he announced as if I would not notice, "and this is how you cook a steak." He slapped the meat into a volcano-hot cast iron pan. The kitchen immediately roiled in black smoke, first setting off the smoke alarm in the kitchen and then every alarm in the house in successive order of distance from the stove, causing a neighbor to call the fire department.

This, I've found in my research, is a fundamental characteristic mentioned in nearly every response from my informants. The burners on a stove have only one setting, and that one is High. I mean, why waste time waiting for pots and pans to slowly heat up to a high temp when you can do it in a fraction of the time with the twist of a wrist?

Another commonly held observation involves the topic of quantity. My balanced and verified survey indicated males (do I *have* to qualify this by saying "some males?) cook meals as if:

A. It is the last meal they will ever eat, so it has to be big enough to face a Velociraptor.

B. Leftovers are a gift to the person who'll be cooking for the remainder of the week and into the next. And, who doesn't love pasta that's the consistency of Amazon packaging?

C. Anything found in the refrigerator can be used with enough flavoring to hide age or appearance.

Moving on to unfair generalization number three, there is consensus that an underlying goal of men in the kitchen is to use every pot, pan, spatula, serving plate, and clean fork in the kitchen. Those thoughtful few who do not leave the countertops strewn with the aforementioned tools will build a precipitous mountain of stainless steel pots and breakable china near the sink because she-who-did-not-cook will surely do the clean-up. It's only fair.

I did have a couple of unique kitchen behaviors reported. One from a woman whose spouse briefly worked in a roomy commercial kitchen. She writes: "They taught him to stop dead in his tracks when encountering another person. This means that when I am also walking in our normal-size kitchen, he slams on his brakes, and I slam right into him. One of us ends up dropping something." It may also be why the commercial cook thing didn't work out, and the husband is now an insurance agent.

And from closer to home, I have an avid cook in my kitchen (NOT COMPLAINING, DEAR) who has set off the smoke alarm more times than I can count. This is, of course, related to observation #1 regarding high heat. However, my personal chef, who also once worked in a commercial kitchen (note observation #7), occasionally places combustible items too near a live burner (picture a paper towel). This results in an actual fire, and I'm thankful the sink is within arm's reach of the stove in our kitchen. He also tells me that it's commonplace for professionals to lay a hot pad atop the lid of a pot on an open flame. Fire extinguisher under sink, always.

And finally (but not comprehensively), there is the innocent, hard-working victim of the male-made meal: the stove. This is particularly evident on a gas stove where burners and tiny parts are receptacles for grease and food particles. Of course, any kind of sauce becomes a viscous pond that transforms into glue when it cools. Some cooks even have a gift for combining ingredients that would be of interest to the space program.

With this blog, I foresee a hiatus in my husband's eagerness to cook for me. But, I feel committed to my informants, who trusted me to report observations that are generally not said out loud. The relief of having someone else cook is cherished. Not worth the risk of complaining. So, with this blog, I sacrifice to the sisterhood of silent acceptance.

Small Town Values, Big Time Grit

Life delivers plenty of extremes – from the catastrophic and global to daily and personal challenges. Recently, we've all suffered with Syria and Turkey - a disaster bigger than our imagination, and we feel helpless to help.

Events in our own lives may seem trivial compared to the enormity of global disasters, but they can be nonetheless daunting enough to send us into a spiral of despair, even surrender. But some folks rise above such trials. I want to tell you about just one of those families I've watched endure and conquer challenges that would lead others to douse their dreams in a river of tears.

The California town of Pollock Pines is a pitstop for vacationers on their way to the High Sierra and home to about 4000 residents. It includes several smaller communities tucked away in neighborhoods scattered across thousands of pine-studded acres for folks who prefer quiet and elbow room to convenience and amenities. Its claim to fame? The main road that runs through Pollock Pines once carried Pony Express riders across the Sierra Nevada and into California in the 1800s.

Today it has a few essential shops – a supermarket, drugstore, hardware store, gas station, and a scattering of smaller businesses. Among them is a historic restaurant that's been part of the community since 1930. The 50 Grand started out as a modest grocery store to serve local lumbering families and later expanded to include a café and other services. The name reflects the restaurant's proximity to Highway 50 and "Grand" because the owners felt their little town was 'A grand place to live.'

Almost 80 years later, the 50 Grand was still serving up dinners and entertaining locals at the bar – but the years had taken a toll. In 2018, Jim and Kim McCarthy picked up the reins of the landmark dining house, perked up the decades-old menu, and infused it with new life. They planned to make gradual changes to remodel and upgrades as time allowed.

"Jim and I looked at the building and thought it would be nice to give the old gal a facelift," says Kim. "There are several generations that have 50 Grand as part of every memory, happy to sad. We wanted to give the town new memories." A new menu, some tidying up, and plans for other changes brought folks in and started a new chapter for the old landmark.

And then came the pandemic. As relatively new owners of the restaurant, it might have been natural to think of the sudden, long-term closure as a dark omen. But the McCarthy family chose to focus on the opportunity that an empty 50 Grand and lots of time (and investment) would offer. They kicked their remodel plans into high gear. Here's a short list from Kim of upgrades and changes accomplished over the long COVID haul:

"We tore the inside flooring down to the dirt ….. There is all new plumbing, electrical, and ventilation … The dining room has new windows, lights, paint, decorations, tables … The bar has new floors, new lights, new back bar (made from the pillars of the old Camino Mill) … The kitchen is huge and new head to toe, front to back - from new equipment to new flooring."

This impressive partial list would be remarkable under the best of circumstances – but the McCarthy family wasn't about to have it easy. I followed Kim's reports on social media and with personal chats. Here, in a list that's inadequate to express the gravity of events that rained down on her family, is what life inside the pandemic delivered: Kim nursed her mother through a cruel disease that claimed her life. Kim's treasured aunt passed away shortly after. The family's beloved dog (a German Shorthair Pointer) died. Most of the staff (along with Kim) got COVID, and their chef had a heart attack. If that wasn't enough bad karma, the McCarthy family was evacuated during the Caldor Fire and camped in a travel trailer in the parking lot of a local church, watching the trajectory of the 225,000-acre fire threaten both their home and the 50 Grand.

Still, throughout the pandemic closure and the year that followed, the family and their construction crew (largely comprised of former restaurant staff) remained committed. Jim McCarthy, a systems engineer by profession, brought extensive knowledge of remodeling, management, and leadership to the effort. Their sons, Quinn and Logan, learned on-the-job construction skills and worked at whatever was needed. Bar manager and mixologist Jimmy Voekler clocked in daily to do so much remodeling that Kim says he could now get his contractor's license. It was a virtual village of helpers, believers, families, and fans who, in the fall of 2022, opened the doors and invited the community back in to dine, drink, and celebrate.

Remodeled and shining like a new silver dollar, the 50 Grand is back in business despite many formidable roadblocks. The exterior got a gentle facelift that preserved its historic façade. Inside, changes are apparent but respectful to the origins of the 50 Grand. Photos of the mountain environment (taken by a talented local photographer) hang on the dining room walls, and memorabilia from the restaurant's long history are polished up and proudly on display. The original neon sign glows brightly in the bar. Former staff is again employed, and new employees are on board.

"Jim and I look at the 50 Grand family ... as family. Though technically staff, we're all on this journey together. We wanted a place that gave local residents a chance to get a job that paid well, a job that could provide benefits. This is unheard of in the service industry." Says Kim. "As we grow, the 50-G family will grow with us. "

What brought the McCarthy personal and professional family through events that would crush the resolve of most people? I think it's the family's uncommon resilience and commitment. The ability to endure pain and yet believe in a better future for the place they call home. And then there's the family's sense of responsibility to the community they serve.

"Jim and I both felt that in the modernization of buildings, people don't take into account the sensory attachment people have with walking into a familiar building and 'remembering when." Explains Kim. "We wanted to keep that for our small town, and for that matter, for people who have adopted this restaurant as their own as they travel through with their families, just as their parents and grandparents   did."
When the McCarthys look back at two years in which they endured great personal loss and pain, the memory is counter-balanced by accomplishment and a purpose fulfilled. Kim explains it this way, "We wake up every day knowing how lucky we are ... There is a belief that when we leave this earth (not anytime soon), we are leaving something behind that is better than when we got here. Leaning on each other and building each other up is the only option for true success. Together, we make a difference.

This month marks the 80th anniversary of the 50 Grand. It's all dressed up for the occasion and ready to serve the community for decades to come. Best of all, it's in the hands of people who endure, overcome, and keep their promises.

The Mind-Body-Stress Connect

My entry into the graduate class of Life happened over the past summer. I turned 77, and two weeks later, this happened:

We reluctantly decided we needed to move from our much loved home at 4000 feet tucked under Cedar trees and nature's many gifts to be closer to the State Capitol, where my husband works as an advocate for mental health. I said goodbye to the deer that visited my bird feeders and trimmed my grass. And to friendly squirrels that came to our yard for daily treats – a few bold enough to sit and beg for peanuts. And to the empty and quiet winding roads where I took Murphy on his daily walks.

Our house sold fast, and due to a bad real estate market, we bought a place that was a big compromise in quality and brimming with hidden challenges we continue to discover. The brighter side? It's in a sweet Gold Rush town closer to the state capitol, but, thankfully, not in the capitol city.

I exhausted all my emotional and physical reserves with the process of moving. The result was an overload of work and worry that I didn't recognize because I've always risen to challenges. But this effort was overtaken by a thing called stress – an emotion that sometimes inspires and other times overwhelms. I got the 'overwhelm' for months after the move. I was crabby, tired, and bummed until I understood my natural response to unwelcome change and extreme demands on both mind and body.

Research on the impacts of stress helped me slowly climb out of the swamp. It also helped that, like lots of people raised Catholic, I was aware of far greater suffering all over the world – and that burden diminished my self-pity. It was also the metaphorical "Starving children in China" my grandmother reminded me of as a child that's imprinted on my soul. And finally, I had you to talk with through it all - a few hours thinking, writing, editing and communicating.

In retrospect, I learned a lot about mind and body – and changes over time. I'm hoping that sharing a few of those stress-induced discoveries might be useful should you find yourself facing similar challenges.

An essential culprit in debilitating stress is cortisol. On a good day, this stress hormone helps control our moods – from motivation to fear. It's sometimes called "nature's alarm system." On bad days, cortisol release can bring on high anxiety, depression, memory loss, digestive problems, and brain fog. I can attest to experiencing each of these in addition to the opposite of one symptom – weight gain. I lost 13 pounds within three weeks without dieting. So, a good thing to know is that if we listen closely to what the body tells us, the brain might get a clue about what we need to do. Stop, slow down, breathe, take a break, get some help.

The negative physical and psychological impacts of extreme stress can affect us at any age but might be more debilitating to older folks who are experiencing other losses and health concerns. (This was not, I'm pleased to report, relevant in my case). However, through the entire moving, packing, losing, and hauling experience, I did fail to take care of myself. Here are a few guidelines I ignored:

Under extreme stress, we're advised to eat better and wiser. *Me – who cooks when you can't remember which box contains silverware?*

Take deep, slow breaths. *On a good day, this approach is too boring and time-consuming for me to adopt.*

Reduce caffeine intake. *What? Haul boxes without a quick and legal fix?*

Exercise – *Just what do you call climbing stairs with an armload of boxes?*

In short (and seriously), there are plenty of ways to counteract stress – all we need is awareness of what's happening (I had none of that) and prioritizing mental and physical well-being.

Interestingly, researchers say that being older may actually be an advantage in dealing with stress. They say that some of us have already experienced loss, challenges, and change. We've developed resiliency and may be able to bounce back faster than the younger set.

Stress isn't like having a headache or breaking a bone because we experience stress in normal everyday life. It's like a background noise that we handle without conscious effort. Stress can also lead to inspiration, problem-solving, and creativity. Moderate stress may stimulate the brain to solve problems. It can spark the growth of stem cells that improve memory and enhance survival. Think how vital stress was to the development of early humans – constant awareness that a saber-toothed tiger might be lurking in the weeds – sizing you and yours for dinner.

But stress that overwhelms can have the opposite effect. Causing forgetfulness and anxiety and suppressing our survival instincts. Researchers also say extreme stress hormone levels appear heritable. For example, children of Holocaust survivors were born with high cortisol levels.

My personal takeaway is that awareness and attention to mind and body under high stress *is* a survival skill. Knowing that something is not wrong with our bodies and brains but that both need our attention.

Six months after the move, I'm feeling more like my old self. Able to recognize opportunities I didn't have in our previous environment – like diverse people, restaurants, movie theatres, and a Home Depot five minutes away. But more important than that? We've got families of deer that visit our yard daily to dine on grass and leaves. And even better, I'm building rapport with squirrels (watching them as I write this) happily dining on peanuts and looking at me through the window, begging for more.

Here's a thought I've adapted from a quotable person; "Sometimes it's the small and simple things like the scent of the rain, the sound of a loved one's voice or happy squirrels that bring us peace." How might you personalize this simple advice?

Painting Happiness
One House at a Time

Before you actually lay eyes on Ronnie Madison, you'll likely hear him. A wide-open laugh comes from his soul and bursts out in an echo of pure happiness that elevates everyone in hearing distance. If you don't immediately join in – well then, time to check your pulse for signs of life.

Ronnie is a house painter by trade and tradition. His father painted homes for 50 years up here in our small, forested communities. And the tradition lives on. His son, Jared, is a local pro whose son, Isaac, completes the family team along with Chance, a red-haired young man who's been unofficially adopted into the Madison fold. Four generations of commitment to a time-honored trade.

We hired Ronnie to paint our previous home encircled by towering cedar trees. Me wanting a change from a baby-poop tan to something more vibrant and exciting. Ronnie warning me the deep forest green I'd chosen was "Pretty dark, Hon. Are you sure?" So, first, Ronnie is the only living male who gets to call me "Hon," and secondly, he ended up extremely pleased with the final results. And when I asked him to paint a few strip pieces with a touch of violet, he gasped and painted despite his doubt – a harmony of nature's colors – green, soft gold, and purple, the color of blooming lavender.

We stood together in front of the rejuvenated house. Ronnie taking it all in. "I tell you, I am surprised. That looks good. Very good! So good, I'm gonna tell everybody it was my idea!" And he threw a great laugh out into the sunshine, making all of us within earshot laugh along.

Ronnie is great at his trade for one simple reason – he absolutely loves painting houses. "Because at the end of the day, you've got something to show for all your work." He says. "You can stand back and look at what you've done. What you've accomplished. And you've put a smile on somebody's face. And then they hand you money. It don't get any better than that!" (This last quip sends Ronnie into another hearty 'guffaw').

But this robust tradesman is deeply committed to a business model that's anchored by integrity and an honest day's work. The kind of work that once characterized the home building and improvement trade when his own dad, Robert, headed up a crew that included a very young Ronnie. At age 12, he remembers feeling less than positive about helping out. He saw agemates having fun while he cleaned paintbrushes and hustled for his dad's crew. But

208

even as a kid, Ronnie had his eye on the prize. "While my friends were playing, I was able to earn money and get a bike and other things that I enjoyed. It was all a good lesson, and I wouldn't have it any other way,"

Ronnie's dad passed away at a young age, and his Mom, Priscilla, grabbed the brushes. But first, there was a tough test to qualify as a trade and paint carpenter. Though she'd been around the trade for most of her adult life, parts of the exam – like a tough section on labor law - she'd never had to learn. However, Ronnie says there was no time for study, and his mom dove in. "She passed all those tests with flying colors," he says with pride. "She kept the business going for 20 more years." And Ronnie paid attention, officially taking Madison Painting into a new era.

He remembers those past decades with a mix of feelings. "People used to take a lot more pride back in the day when they built homes," he says. "Not like now. I've done repainting on some of those custom homes, and it's just shoddy work. They just throw stuff together and sell it fast."

Ronnie's latest job was finished today - our new house in the charming town of Placerville, CA. We'd traded our grand home in the forest for a modest house on a hill within walking distance of the Gold Rush city that puts us closer to my husband's work at the State Capitol. Unlike our mountain home, the new place lacked character and color – a condition I was sure we could remedy with Ronnie's help. For me, paint was a priority because both the interior and exterior were painted gray – that is, in my colorful mind – the shade of satin lining in a coffin. It had to go – and quickly! It's now replaced with a deep verdant green outside – inside with walls of peach and apricot and a fresh lime green. When Ronnie heard my plan, he was unsurprised. "I know better than to question those color choices," he said to his crew, remembering how he'd advised against my prior color combos and later bragged about the results. "That looks so good; I think I'll tell people it was my idea!" he says and busts out another happy howl.

Having his crew here for much of the past week was an antidote for the tortures of moving. The packing, hauling, storing, lugging, unpacking, and other physical and mental challenges that can't ever be described as fun. But with Ronnie erupting with contagious laughter, my days brightened.

Being around people who love their work and each other's company and deeply believe in the value of a good day's work is contagious. Ronnie Madison is a master of spreading upbeat vibes while guiding his team to customer satisfaction. But his positive approach is not a business tactic – it's his nature, passed down and along through generations.

With the job done, I'm already missing the regular punctuation of his signature laugh that sets off a chain of laughter. How does he remain so pleased with his trade? I think it's in the Madison DNA. "When we paint somebody's house, it's just so satisfying," he says. "When we're done with a job, and the owner is excited about it, that's what we work for," he says. "It makes me feel so good to make people happy."

Banking on a Memory

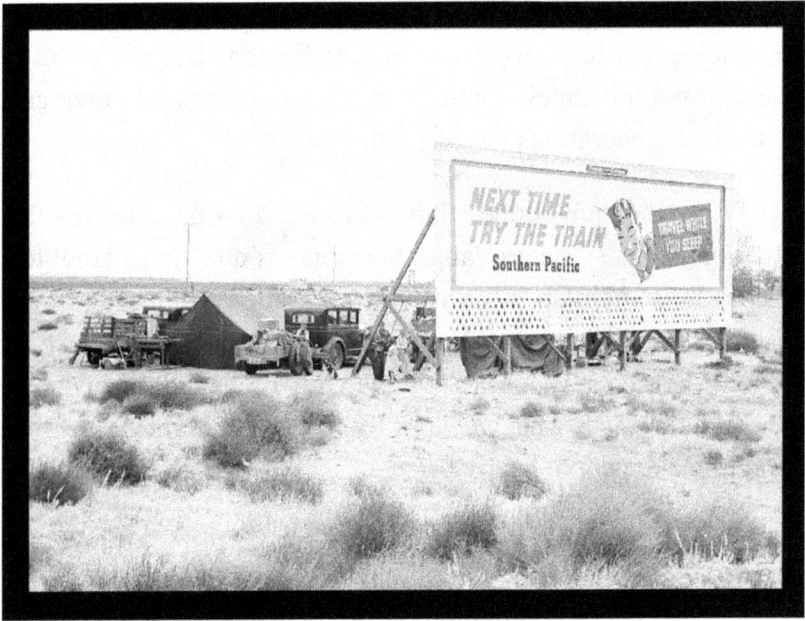

I met a powerful man over a decade ago. I've not written about him because he's admonished me countless times – "I don't like to read about me ... or talk about me. That's just the way that I am." So, I'll honor that by changing his name to Larry.

I first met him when he was a major player in banking and finance. He hired me to do some freelance writing for him. I initially thought I'd be writing about (yawn) banking, But no. He wanted me to write about programs that helped people experiencing hard times – homeless folks and those in shelters around our county. I soon discovered that's where his heart lived, as he used his extraordinary business skills to do high-dollar banking deals from an executive office in California's capital city.

His own story started in the Dust Bowl era when his family packed up the car and made the journey west on Route 66 from drought-ridden Arkansas to Needles, California. There, they joined the flood of desperate migrants, hoping the state held salvation and the promise of a better future for their families. Larry was only a young boy, but he remembers nights spent sleeping in roadside ditches and late afternoons under the shade of highway billboards that admonished, "Oakies, Go Home."

Once over the high pass into southern California, Larry's family found work together as migrant farm labor, following crops up and down the state. Sleeping in tents, on the move with the crops in season, and, eventually, finding a one-room cabin in a makeshift migrant camp near Bakersfield. Like countless children of the Dust Bowl, Larry attended elementary school sporadically because work sent his family traveling up and down the Golden State. Even as a young child, he joined the adults in the field. Crops like cotton, grapes, and fruit trees sent migrants to distant parts of the state. Families spent nights in cars, tents, and irrigation ditches, anywhere deemed safe – no shelters were provided. Eventually, Larry's family settled in a small desert town near Bakersfield with a nearby school, some simple resources, and farmwork that didn't force them to pack up and hit the road for weeks and months on end.

It was a hand-to-mouth life. Material pleasures were few, but Larry's extended family brought a priceless tradition with them - their love of traditional country music, guitars, fiddles, and their voices. They sang songs that honored simple values – like family, faith, and the hope for a better tomorrow. After long, hard days in fields and furrows, his family joined neighbors to fill hot summer nights with songs and memories – sending tunes from the Great Plains out into the darkening sky.

When Larry was old enough to work on his own, Willah Stacy, owner of the General Store in Thornton, hired him to do a few odd jobs. At the same time, he was finally able to attend school on a regular basis. There, he met Don McCormick, a seventh-grade teacher who took a special interest in Larry's education He taught and mentored him. Instilled an awareness that school was a brass ring to success in California. Larry grabbed it and set his future in motion.

Once out of school, he got his first job in a local bank, thanks again to Willah Stacy. He started modestly with a broom and cleaning supplies. But, little by little, Larry was given more responsibility and opportunities to learn the baking trade.

He rose fast and high, drinking in education and opportunities provided by folks who believed in him. Each of them became a cherished memory as Larry learned, climbed, and proved himself worthy of their support. He never forgot where he came from and who gave him wings to fly.

Along with gratitude to folks who set him on his professional path, Larry also honored his family's tradition of playing music. It's been a background for his journey from migrant camps to high finance and into active retirement – the old-time fiddle tunes and country songs of childhood. He's cut some records with friends and requires no prompting to pick up a guitar and play. A fine Martin even leaned against a wall in Larry's high-rise office. I felt honored to listen to a tune now and then – though country music was an anachronism in the high-rise environment. But Larry's pure Nashville voice (as good as any I've heard on recordings) was – and is – a pleasure to hear.

Larry retired from banking several years ago. But he'll never retire from his personal mission to honor folks where they are in life. Making his rounds along the river bank, he treats the down-and-out with the same dignity he affords to friends and associates. If the moment is right, he hands over some cash to help people make it through another day. He's tapped friends and neighbors who are happy to make donations to his personal outreach and adds his own cash. He doesn't talk about these treks. Likes to stay under the radar.

I consider myself lucky to have met Larry so many years ago. There are few people like him. From a historic era in American history when nothing was easy, most things were physical, and few people soared to the heights of opportunity, Larry's story is worth sharing, even though I may get fired for doing it. But I believe good people ought to be celebrated and recognized. Larry (again, not his real name) has been on my list for too long.

Waves in Time

It is a sun-filled day, and heat rises from the sand on the beach. Of course, being Frinton on Sea and facing the English Channel, there is still a nip of crispness in the air. There are few people here with me, and the cove seems intensely personal. This sense of solace does not change when a middle-aged couple slowly climbs down the rock stairs from the sea wall above and stands on the sand. They pause there, looking out, and I wonder if they will merely rest a while and leave. They look like tourists to the coast, a little surprised to find themselves here.

They are not dressed for the beach. She wears a pale blue sweater set and navy slacks. Her shoes have low heels. She holds a worn brown purse over her shoulder. He seems dressed for work in a white shirt and grey pants. Two pens protrude from the pocket of his shirt, and he unbuttons the sleeves and rolls them up a bit. They are not far from where I sit, book and camera in hand.

He says something softly to her, and she shakes her head. "No, I'll just stay here. You go ahead. I'd ruin my shoes," she tells him.

"Take them off," he suggests, smiling, playful.

She gives him a look of exasperation and waves him off like a mischievous puppy. Her hair is a chestnut color, likely covering a crop of unwanted grey. It has been recently styled, and she tries to pat it back into place as the breeze plays with it. After riffling in her purse, she pulls a thin white scarf out and ties it loosely around her head.

Her husband removes his shoes, drops them in the sand, and strolls to the water's edge. He glances back at her, watching the ritual of saving her hair-do. His eyes are deeply blue, like a fisherman's, and his face is etched with lines. I know this man is not a fisherman. His countenance hints of a desk job from which he is perhaps retired. Nonetheless, I picture him at ease here, alongside the sea, drawn to it almost without choice. I know he will wade in the water.

He walks beyond the damp line where the waves lap the shore. The man with hair the color of sea foam rolls up the legs of his pants and wanders in. His ankles are white as limestone. They are soon covered by water that laps up to his knees.

He stands and stares out over the Channel, his hands thrust into the pockets of his pants. He looks far southeast, and I wonder if he is reaching for memories of a week he'd spent at the beach long ago when he was young and full. He turns slightly as if to leave but pauses instead and inches further into the tumbling surf.

After many minutes lost in his thoughts, he slowly walks back to his wife who still stands on the stairs by the sea wall clutching her purse to her chest. "Come in with me?" he urges with a faint smile.

"I don't have a towel in the car," she answers, clearly unwilling to join her husband in his rite with the water. "Go ahead. Don't worry about me."

He takes off his watch and hands it to his wife. He turns his back to her again and walks directly into the water, the forward thrust splashing his trousers, making dark, wet spots. The surf is gentle and laps up against legs so thin they look as if they might snap if hit by a strong wave.

Behind him, on the beach, two lovers lay entwined on a red blanket pressed into the sand like a nest. The young woman with hair the color of honey quickly sits up and laughs at some words she and her lover have shared. The sound peals like a bell, riding over the sand and out to sea. Her long hair dances in the wind, and she runs her fingers through it. The man reaches up and grabs her arm, pulling her down against him again until they are wrapped around each other, touching from toe to head. They are dressed for touching; she wearing a deep backless swimsuit, and he in brief trunks that shimmer when he moves.

The older man wrests his gaze from the horizon and turns to look at his wife.

"It's warm," he shouts over the low roar of the surf and the laughter of the young couple. "It's not at all cold!"

His wife shifts her purse to her hip, raises her chin, and answers, "That's nice," still not drawn to join him in his baptism of salt and foam. She will stand patiently, without complaint, and wait until her husband tires of the moment. He is quite wet by now, and she waves at him in a gesture of tolerance for his frivolity. She shakes her head slightly, like a mother watching a precocious child.

218

As the man looks at his wife and she at him, his gaze falls upon the young couple in the sand. He is of a generation that is loathe to stare, but he watches them nonetheless. I see his chest rise and fall in a great exaggerated sigh. The look on his face is not disapproving but softly sorrowful. His wife has pinched her mouth up like a closed blossom. She gives no sign she's seen the young couple at all, though I know she has glanced, perhaps more than once. She gazes briefly at me and then up at the sea wall and back out to the water.

The young lovers are oblivious to the older couple. Oblivious, in fact, to everything save their mutual bodies and fervor for each other. They roll over so she is now on top, her hair caressing her lover's face like strands of windblown silk. His arms, flecked with tiny grains of sand, shimmer in the sunlight as he moves his hands over her bare back. I wonder what stops them from coupling there on the beach in front of us, each with our own reflections.

The husband reaches down and scoops up a handful of water. He wipes his face and lets the drops fall to his white shirt. I see him taste the salt on his lips before turning and facing the endless sea. His wife's eyes drift fully to the lovers, and she watches them with curiosity. Her head is tilted to one side, and her lips are slightly parted as if preparing to ask a question.

The day has been uncharacteristically bright and warm, but clouds have gathered and now obscure the late afternoon sun. Without the sun's reflection on the sand, the beach loses its warmth. It is a signal for the husband to turn his back on the eastern horizon and allow his legs to dry in the breeze.

He pushes his way through the waves, past the young couple, digging his toes into the sand as he walks to his wife's side. They stand together for a moment, looking out at the sea, over the lovers who seem unaware of the change in climate. Where they touch each other, there is no room for chill; they are an envelope of warmth defying the passage of time, of temperature, perhaps, even the turning of the earth.

The husband puts his arm around his wife's shoulder. "Cold?" he asks.

"Getting there," she answers. "Back to the car then?" She hands him his watch and helps him fasten it around his wrist. He watches her face as she tucks away the loose end of the band. They turn and climb the worn stairs of the seawall to the cliffs above. I follow at a distance and listen. Wanting something for them, from them.

They don't talk as they walk the path along the seawall edge. There are wildflowers here and there, and benches built of weathered wood overlook the expansive view of the Channel. They pause at one bearing an inscription etched in brass. It is the woman's voice. "In loving memory of my husband and friend, Len Cherry, whose eyes were as blue as the sea and heart as deep."

"Yes, well," said the man, looking out at the half circle of sun peeking from the clouds and touching the back of the bench with warm light. "He must have been quite a fellow."

His wife, feeling the bite of the wind and looking into his eyes, answers by hooking her arm in his and pulling her husband closer. She looks up into his eyes and smiles. "Come on. Let's get you to the car. You're soaked. "

I rest on Len Cherry's bench and watch the young lovers sit up and gaze out to sea. The clouds have parted. The waning sun hits them, and their bodies cast long shadows in the sand.

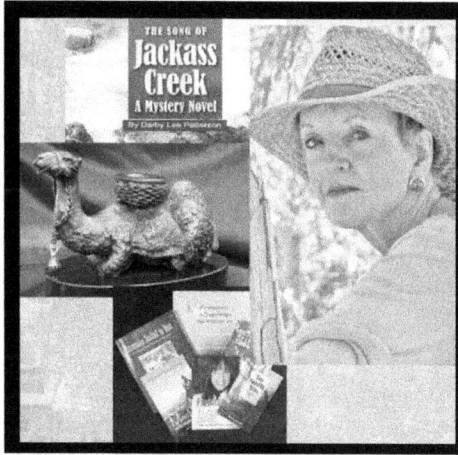

Comments, Questions?

darby@darbypatterson.com

Mystery Lover? Check out

"The Song of Jackass Creek:

4.5 Amazon Stars

By Darby Patterson

www.ingramcontent.com/pod-product-compliance
Lightning Source LLC
Chambersburg PA
CBHW061015280326
41935CB00009B/975